WELL I'LL BE HANGED

TIM DEMPSEY

SUNBURY PRESS

Mechanicsburg, Pennsylvania   USA

Published by Sunbury Press, Inc.
50 West Main Street, Suite A
Mechanicsburg, Pennsylvania 17055

www.sunburypress.com

For information about special discounts for bulk purchases, please contact Sunbury Press Orders Dept. at (855) 338-8359 or orders@sunburypress.com.

To request one of our authors for speaking engagements or book signings, please contact Sunbury Press Publicity Dept. at publicity@sunburypress.com.

ISBN: 978-1-62006-336-1 (Trade Paperback)

FIRST SUNBURY PRESS EDITION: May 2014

Product of the United States of America
0 1 1 2 3 5 8 13 21 34 55

Set in Bookman Old Style
Designed by Lawrence Knorr
Cover by Lawrence Knorr
Edited by Angela Wagner

Continue the Enlightenment!

DEDICATION

This book is dedicated to Doctors Thomas Langdon, S. George Sojka, Michael Peters, Michael Dehning, Harry Klein, Nurse Practitioner Suzanna Harrington, "Big Ron," and the nurses and staff of Omaha's Methodist Hospital who were all responsible for giving me the gift of time needed to finish this book, and also to my loving wife Jill who encouraged me to take the risk.

TABLE OF CONTENTS

PREFACE
and
ACKNOWLEDGMENTS

During the interview process, candidates applying for positions as law enforcement officers are generally asked if they have given consideration to the fact that they may be required to take a life in the line of duty. For most, it's the last time they will talk about the issue. The concern, however, is on the mind of many from the day they are hired to the day they retire. In my 37 years in law enforcement, I was one of the fortunate officers who made it through their career without having to do so. That's not to say, however, that I didn't face the decision more than once. Some friends and co-workers were not so lucky. Most everyone in law enforcement familiar with the aftermath of such an incident will agree that, despite outward signs of being unaffected, that is not the case. Justifiable homicide is much easier for our legislatures and courts to rationalize than it is for a peace officer in his or her mind.

Today, the majority of officer involved deaths are a result of volatile situations, and the decision to shoot is made in a split second. Therefore, the officer deals with the incident after the fact. Historically speaking, however, that was not always the case. In Nebraska, before 1901, it was the job of an elected county sheriff to preside over the legal execution of anyone convicted in their county for a capital crime. In 1981, I read an account of an execution, which occurred at the Douglas County Courthouse in 1891. At that time, I vividly remember thinking that the sheriff's task must have been a daunting one, and I couldn't help imagining that he must have agonized over such a protracted process.

After I retired in 2007, I revisited the facts surrounding the 1891 hanging. I found my assumption to be correct. The sheriff in the case found the task of hanging another person very distasteful, to say the least. It was also obvious that because the sheriff was the long time custodian of the condemned man, the act of hanging him took on an even greater burden. His interaction simply created a familiarity with him, and the execution became personal.

I decided to look at the three other executions at the Douglas County courthouse to see how those lawmen handled their tasks. I was sure that news accounts could yield clues regarding how the two other sheriffs and one United States Marshal felt about doing the job of executioner. In all the cases it was clearly apparent that they all shared the same aversion to that particular part of their job.

In reading the accounts, I found something else intriguing. The only similarity in the four cases was the fact that they ended at the gallows. I realized that in today's world, only two of the men would have possibly been sentenced to death. I decided to look at the other 9 Nebraska cases in which the county sheriff was called upon to perform the gruesome task. In addition to searching news accounts, I traveled to many of the jurisdictions and reviewed court files and library records. I was pleased and surprised to find that many of the original files were in pristine condition and accessible. The results of my review indicated a strong similarity in how each sheriff felt about being an executioner. I found each case to be extremely interesting and decided to share my results in this manuscript.

I would like to acknowledge the assistance of the following persons for their help in making this work possible: Mary Lou Kristensen and the Kearney County Historical Society; Seward Public Library, Lana Urban and other employees of Seward County Clerk of the District Court's office; Caryl Colson and the Clerk of the Polk County District Court; April Stevens, Director of the Osceola Public Library; Debra Hume, Clerk of the Cheyenne County District Court, Lesa Arterburn, Rita Clawson, and the Gage County Historical Museum; Barbara Hegr, Lavonda Bando, and the staff of Nebraska City's Morton-James Public Library; Janet Davenport and the staff of the Keene Library in Fremont; Lynette Bendig and the Dodge County Clerk of the District Court's office; Lorana Eggert and the Cherry County Clerk of the District Court's office; Mary-Jo Miller of the Nebraska State Historical Society; Harlan Seyfer, Plattsmouth Nebraska Historian; Gary Rosenberg and the Douglas County Historical Society; the reference staff at the Omaha Public Library; Jeannene Douglas and former Director Bob Houston of the Nebraska Department of Corrections; Coi Drummond-Gehrig and the Denver Public Library; and Joyce Burner and the National Federal Archives. A special appreciation is extended to Jon Blecha and Jill Lustgarten for their help in editing this work.

Lastly, I need to thank Wildcat Jim, a Wyoming Territory desperado that met his fate by a vigilance committee in 1898. The coroner and the sheriff of the town were asked by the district judge to look into the case. At the inquest, several members of the committee testified that they found Wildcat lying in the street, and since it was 30° below zero, they were forced to place a rope around his neck and lift him up to save him from being frozen.

Unfortunately, they said he perished in their courageous attempts to save him. The coroner sent in his report. A few days later a judgment arrived from the court. It said, "Dear Sir — the finding of the jury has been received and filed. It was a peculiar case. There was a similar one in Texas a few years ago. The jury there, however, leaned to the opinion that the deceased had come to death from fright, due to a premonition of sudden death." After reading the court's finding, the sheriff, according *The Kansas City Journal*, was heard to say, "Well, I'll be hanged."[1]

---

1 *The Kansas City Journal*, February 6, 1898

INTRODUCTION

During the frontier days in Nebraska Territory, outlaws plying their trade often found justice to be as swift as it was sure. Nowhere was this fact more evident than in the far southeastern part of the Territory. On December 2 in 1854, for example, three inept horse thieves landed themselves in the makeshift jail at Brownville. The small town is just about as far east and south as you can go in Nebraska. A vigilance committee from the town decided to pay a visit to the jail, and in the early morning hours escorted the desperados to the middle of a frozen Missouri River.[1] The concerned citizens found a large air hole in the ice, and the three shackled prisoners were forced to kneel at the water's edge and allowed a few minutes to pray. Their introspection was cut short by the impatient vigilantes, however, and they trio was forcibly pushed into the raging current. Reports said that the horse thieves tried desperately to hang on to the edge of the ice while simultaneously swearing at the vigilantes. Committee members responded by stomping their fingers with the intent of hastening the departure of the cobbled crooks downstream. The men eventually were forced to let go. They were swept away by the fast moving current, but not before some collateral damage occurred. One of the stompers was a bit too slow. A soon to be departed desperado grabbed his boot and pulled him into the swirling river. No one knew the identities of the committee members, but quite coincidentally, one of the town's leading business men went missing about the time of the incident and was never heard from again.[2]

Just four years later, another man found out that justice in the Nebraska Territory was sure and swift. Sheriff Wilson Maddox was chasing a horse thief known only by the last name of Leavitt, near Falls City, which is just 25 miles south of Brownsville. The Sheriff eventually captured Leavitt and brought him back to St. Stephen's, a small town on the Missouri River in what is now Richardson County.[3] The leaders of a regulator committee decided to conduct an impromptu trial. With the sheriff in attendance, a large crowd estimated at 200 people stood by while the evidence was presented. The vigilance society found him guilty and sentenced him to hang. A group from the committee bound

Leavitt, placed him in a wagon, and drove him to a "hollow" just outside of the now defunct St. Stephens. The group found a stout tree and tossed the rope over its strongest limb. They forced Leavitt to stand on a box in the back of the wagon, and when he obliged, they simply drove the team away. Leavitt's body was left hanging for an entire day, making his justice sure, swift, and very public.[4]

In 1867, Nebraska achieved statehood, and the old portion of the southeast Territory was defined by several new counties, one of which is Otoe County. Nebraska City is the county seat of Otoe County and is about 30 miles north of Brownville. On July 22, 1887, a part of County's population became indignant and angry. In the morning, a large crowd witnessed the hanging of David W. Hoffman. Hoffman was considered dastardly because he and a confederate caused a Missouri Pacific passenger train headed to Kansas City from Omaha to derail with a crew and 87 passengers on board, killing the engineer and seriously hurting several others.[5] The fact that Hoffman "got a free pass to Pluto's Domain," did not cool the discontent of the people.[6] They were still fuming because the Otoe County jail also housed Lee Shellenberger, a man the people of that area considered far more dastardly than Hoffman. Shellenberger and his second wife, Marinda, first plotted and then killed Shellenberger's eleven year old daughter, Maggie, in the basement of their farmstead. They slit her throat from ear to ear, and evidence showed that it was a botched job causing the little girl to suffer horribly because of their ineptitude.[7] Emma, Maggie's natural mother, died and left Maggie valuable land, which her father and stepmother wanted for themselves. Their lust for the land prompted the pair to hatch a plot to kill the child and try to conceal their crime by asserting that the child committed suicide. The scheme unraveled at the coroner's inquest, and the two were quickly considered suspects.[8] Lee and Marinda were tried separately. Lee was convicted and sentenced to hang while his wife awaited trial. Lee was housed in the Otoe County jail, while Marinda, because of a change in venue, was in the Lancaster County jail at Lincoln. Hoffman's execution didn't ease the community's tensions, and as a matter of fact, it intensified the rage of many in Otoe County who wanted to see justice done. Hoffman's execution was actually the spark that lit the fuse of bedlam for those that didn't want to delay Shellenberger's send off. On July 23, 1887, "A mob of determined farmers," forced their way into the jail around 1:30 A.M.[9]

"He did not speak a word until he was forced through the hole in the floor, when he cried out, 'Oh God Almighty.' He was pushed and dragged out through the hall and to the foot of a tree not over twenty feet from the front door of the court house, when a man sprung up the tree, rope in hand, and swung it over a limb. Then there was a cry and a shout of 'pull him up.' At first he begged hard for his life, but when he saw the case was hopeless he became very nervy and never faltered once. 'I'll haunt you sons of bitches if I can.' The body was hauled up about eight feet then lowered and the rope fixed better around his neck and then pulled up again."[10] "He was strung up again, and this was repeated until he had been lifted and dropped six times, when he went out for the last time; his life was about gone, anyhow, and he was as limp as if life was gone."[11]

It was speculated that the vigilantes, described by the newspapers, "as a mob of determined farmers," were actually a group of men from Shellenberger's German community. The proof offered for this conjecture was that when the mob was sure they had done their job; they lined up in a military fashion and marched out of the courthouse compound singing a German marching song.[12]

It would be a little over three years later when a similar scene played out 45 miles north in Omaha, Nebraska. Allen Jones and Dorothy Jones were two elderly people in their 70's. In the winter of 1890, the couple did a favor for their son-in-law and tended some livestock housed on a recently purchased farm near Omaha. An ex-convict and drifter, using the alias of Ed Neal, went to the farm and shot and killed the couple, then ingloriously buried them under a pile of manure.

Neal was eventually convicted and sentenced to hang at the Douglas County Jail, where he had been confined there for several months awaiting the results of a legal appeal. On October 9, 1891, several of Omaha's citizens gathered near the courthouse to get a glimpse of Neal's "drop from life.[13]" The hanging took on an almost circus like event, with vendors selling popcorn and apples to the crowd.[14] After the hanging, the majority of the gathering dispersed, but several people stayed and took in the sights of Omaha's downtown. Other stragglers began congregating in groups talking about George Smith, alias Joe Coe, one of the jail's other prominent residents, and the talk wasn't pretty.

On October 7, 1891, the Wednesday before the Neal hanging, Smith, or Joe Coe, who happened to be black, purportedly assaulted a five year old white girl. Coe was arrested by Omaha police, and quickly rumors spread about the incident, including one which was not true, that being, that the little girl had died. Other rumors, which were true, also circulated with telegraph speed. Those rumors related that Coe recently committed a similar crime in Council Bluffs, Iowa, but the case was dismissed because of a jurisdictional technicality.[15] By late evening, the small groups formed a large mob intent on ensuring that Coe would not go unpunished again. Just as the mob had done in Otoe County three years prior, the mob stormed the jail.[16]

In the early hours of October 10, 1891, "Smith (alias Coe) was tied up with one rope and another placed around his neck. At one point he was heard to say, 'You are killing me.'"[17] "A hundred ready hands seized the rope and dragged him to a motor pole (Trolley) at the northeast corner. Smith gasped, 'By G_d I'm Innocent' as the rope tightened. Only those nearest him heard it. Suddenly the wire began to grow taut under the rope. Then, in a bluish glare of the electric arc lights, a head, a pair of shoulders, and then a body, rose out of the dense throng."[18]

The body hung for nearly an hour and then was lowered to the street. The rope used to hang Coe was cut away, leaving only the noose around his neck. Eventually, "it was cut into small pieces" and shared as souvenirs by the lynch mob.[19]

After Coe's lynching, *The Omaha Daily Bee* reported that, "It seems to be a style to have a lynching follow a hanging in Nebraska."[20] The story referred Coe's lynching, Shellenberger's lynching in Otoe County, and an aborted lynching attempt in Polk County in 1885. In the latter case, a crowd of five thousand gathered at Osceola, Nebraska to watch the execution of Milton W. Smith, who was convicted of murdering his wife. The crowd ripped down the barriers near the gallows where Smith was executed. News reports said that the crowd wanted to lynch another man named Gebhardt, who was in jail for the attempted murder of his wife, but the sheriff had prior warning and moved the prisoner.[21]

Immediately after the Shellenberger lynching, his attorney said that both during and after the trial, that there had been several rumors about storming the jail and lynching his client. He said the legal execution of Hoffman was the impetus needed for the mob to form, and actually do it.[22]

About the same time, a faction in the State took up the argument and used the idea of runaway justice to try and abolish capital punishment altogether. For several years, Nebraska's Legislature argued the issue back and forth.[23] In 1895, during the debate on the Bill, State Senators continued to make the point that moving the executions from the communities in which the crime was committed to the State Penitentiary would prevent riots.[24] The issue was finally resolved in the spring of 1901, when the Legislature again considered a measure to make the change. The House version of the Bill was sponsored by Dodge County Representative George L. Loomis from Fremont, Nebraska, who, coincidentally, prosecuted two young men who were hung simultaneously there in 1891. The Bill easily passed and was subsequently passed by the Senate and became law.[25] Although the Bill passed with the emergency clause, which meant that it became

LEE SHELLENBERGER

effective immediately upon the signing by Governor Dietrich, it was not actually used until 1903.[26]

From the beginning of Nebraska's Statehood in 1867, until the change took effect in 1901, Nebraska's county sheriffs were responsible for hanging 13 people in the courtyards of Nebraska's county jails. During the same period, a United States Marshal used Douglas County's gallows to hang a soldier in the jail yard.[27]

The stories of the fourteen people, who literally reached the end of their rope at the hands of a county sheriff, are as varied as their crimes. The consensus of the day, in terms of "just deserts" for the recipients of "the rope," was overwhelming. The evidence shows that more than likely they got what they deserved. In retrospect, however, over a hundred years later, we know that some rewards may not have been all that just, and in some cases, justice maybe a little too swift. What follows are those stories.

Chapter I
Samuel D. Richards
Frontier Serial Killer

In today's world, criminal psychologists would likely say that S. D. Richards was a "dyed in the wool" sociopath, but in 1879, he was simply known as a "bloodthirsty wretch."[28] The *Omaha Herald* in their April 26, 1879 edition also called him, "the Strangest Human Being of this Age."[29] History tells us that any and all disparagements afforded Richards were well earned. He was convicted of only one murder but admitted to as many as 9, including the bludgeoning deaths of a woman and her 3 young children.[30]

The end of the story of 25 year old Samuel D. Richards began with his hanging at Minden, Nebraska, on April 26, 1879. It was one of the first legal executions in the recently created State of Nebraska. Otaway Barker was executed in Omaha on February 14, 1868, but his crime was committed in Omaha on November 23, 1866, when it was still the Nebraska Territory.[31] Richard's execution was attended by estimates of 1,500 to 2,500 people from all of the surrounding area.[32] The affair saw "family after family," arrive in their wagons, and "the day seemed to put on a grand holiday appearance."[33] Rolf Johnson and three of his friends hitched a team to a buggy and drove for six hours just to attend the gala and get a glimpse of the man considered evil incarnate.[34] The event ended up being a mob scene, and was only quelled when Richards was dispatched though the trap door of the gallows into perpetuity.

Kearney County Sheriff Matt Kieran, Richard's executioner, made arrangements to bury Richard's body in a draw a few miles outside of Minden. Hearing rumors of a body snatching, after local doctors were denied requests to perform an autopsy, the sheriff arranged for a guard at the grave.[35] The surveillance only lasted one night, but it wasn't long enough. Richard's remains were unearthed the following night and taken to an abandoned building for a belated post mortem exam.[36] Once the scientific work was done, the body was discarded in such a manner that

The Kearney County Butchery.

The Omaha Bee the gives the following particulars of the murder of Mrs. Harlson and her three children:

It is believed that the families were murdered by a man named SD Richards in order to obtain possession of a span of mules, some grain and a homestead claim.

Mrs. Harlson's head was smashed with a smoothing iron; also, one child killed with the same instrument. One was taken by the heels and had its brains dashed out against the floor. The third child was kicked to death.

Still another murder was committed in Kearney County, the victim being Peter Anderson, who lived about 5 miles from the Harlson's place.

He was found dead in the cellar of his house, under a coal pile. It is thought the deed was done by the same party. He was pounded on the head with a hammer, and was killed for little money had with him at the time.

many of the parts were scattered around Minden, purportedly by the town's dogs.[37] Parts of the skeleton were bleached and retained by one of the doctors who attended Richard's hanging. He also, incidentally, was one of the physicians that pronounced him dead.[38] Probably the most bizarre defilement of Richard's remains was the display of his skull in the window of the *Kearney County Gazette*.[39]

At the time, there was no doubt an absence of human dignity as far as Richard's remains were concerned, what caused the state of indifference is yet another story. The tale of Samuel D. Richards, also known

SAM RICHARDS

as Stephen D. Richards, began in Wheeling, West Virginia on March 18, 1856, the day he was born. His family was poor, and the major influence in his life was his mother, who did her best to raise him as a strict Methodist. When Richards was approximately four years old, the family moved to Ohio and seemed to take on an almost vagabond lifestyle. His father worked as a laborer, and the family moved frequently from place to place within the State of Ohio. The family eventually tried to sink their roots in Mount Pleasant, Ohio, but just about as they were established, Richards' mother died. The death occurred on September's 18th, 1871, when Richards was 15 years old. Family life was almost nonexistent after his mother's death, and he began living an aimless life of working as a farmhand and moving from place to place. The longest job held by Richards was at the State Insane Asylum in Mount Pleasant, where he was an attendant in one of the more violent wards. He would later say that he became acquainted with violence and dead bodies when he worked that job.[40]

In February of 1876, Richards eventually made his way west to the Mississippi River, and spent some time in Burlington, Iowa. He worked as a farmhand, but spent most free evenings at a house of ill repute, where he began associating with a group of older outlaws. They convinced him that life was better out west and that it would be much easier to pass the counterfeit money they helped him to acquire. A few months later, Richards struck out for the west with a good deal of counterfeit money and what he would later refer to as "his shootin' irons."[41]

After traveling across the Missouri River into Nebraska, he traveled first to Hastings, and eventually ended up at what was known at the time as Kearney Junction, in the middle of Nebraska.[42] Kearney Junction was situated along the Platte River and was part of the Oregon Trail located in the Platte Valley. At one time or another, most of the historic characters of the Wild West, including Kit Carson, Wild Bill Hickok, and Calamity Jane, traveled through and spent time in the area.[43]

Richards traveled around what was considered the Kearney area for about two weeks, and one day met a stranger on the road who happened to also be headed to the town of Kearney. The men, both on horseback, chitchatted as they rode for a short while, and then decided to camp. They sat around the campfire, and to break the monotony, decided to play some poker. Richards got lucky and won most of the stranger's money. At first, the man accused Richards of cheating him but let the matter drop. They eventually bedded down for the night, but unbeknownst to Richards, the matter was not settled. In the morning, as the pair resumed their travel, the stranger abruptly stopped his horse and demanded a refund. Richards pulled out his pistol and shot the disgruntled gambler in his left eye, killing him instantly. He took the man's body, dumped it in the Platte River, and proceeded into Kearney, where he sold the stranger's horse.[44]

Richards thought it might be a good idea to let things cool off for a while, so he traveled to Phelps County, just to the south of Kearney. After spending a few days there, he thought the threat had passed and headed back towards Kearney. As he was heading back, he stopped along the road to talk to a man who was on foot. The man asked him if Richards knew the whereabouts of the disgruntled gambler. Richards was surprised to learn that the man's name was John, and that the pedestrian and John were business partners. He made the dreadful mistake of telling Richards he had seen the two together days before when they were headed for Kearney.[45] Richards said he didn't know what happened to John, but being a kind sort, offered the inquisitor the use of his extra horse. The men started for Kearney, and as soon as Richards jockeyed into a position behind the stranger, he shot him in the back of the head. Stranger number two was also killed instantly, and his body left for the buzzards.[46]

Richards decided to head west. He stopped at North Platte, Ogallala, and Sidney in Nebraska, and ended up in Cheyenne, Wyoming. He spent several weeks there, doing not much of anything except gambling, and eventually met two companions who were about to leave for Kansas City. He decided to join them.[47]

After they reached Kansas City, Richards worked as a farmhand on a place just outside of the City for several weeks, and eventually headed back east to Iowa, near Cedar Rapids. He still had a lot of counterfeit money and decided to buy a new buggy and some horses from a young man who was traveling through the area. He paid for buggy and team using the bogus cash, but made the mistake of staying around socializing for a few days. The man discovered that Richards' money was not real, and threatened to have him arrested if he didn't make good on the purchase. Again, unfortunately for the young man, the confrontation took place on the outskirts of Cedar Rapids and away from witnesses. Richards simply shot him and covered his body with brush.[48]

Richards sold the buggy and team and once again headed for Nebraska. He made it past Omaha and ended up in Lincoln in January of 1878. After spending a few weeks in Lincoln, Richards headed back to Kearney with the intention of seeing some friends he met the last time he passed through the State. One of the friends, an unsavory character named Jasper Harelson, lived in Kearney County with his wife and three children. Another of Sam's friends was a man named Underwood, who was purportedly involved in the Big Springs train robbery.[49] Richards found his Nebraska acquaintances in the Buffalo County jail in the town of Kearney and provided them with some tools, with which they used to escape. Richards, who later referred to Jasper Harelson as a "train robber," said that Jasper fled for Texas, leaving his wife and children on their farm. Jasper apparently consorted with some interesting characters. At least 12 outlaws were in the gang that robbed the Union Pacific Express train at Big Springs. The Sam Bass gang was ultimately identified as part of the robbery, but several went unidentified. Some believed Frank and Jesse James were two unidentified men in the robbery, and theorists often support their notion by the fact that Jesse planned on settling down just 50 miles from Kearney shortly before he was killed.[50]

Richards wasn't a part of the robbery, but did find things a little too warm after helping them escape. He headed to Grand

Island, which was then a small town 40 miles to the north and east of Kearney. He spent the next few months there cooling off. In March of 1878, Richards left Grand Island headed back to Kearney in the company of a man known to him only as Gemge. The two men traveled until nightfall and camped for the night, but Richards awoke during the early morning hours and decided to ride on to Kearney. When Gemge was awakened, he was angry at being disturbed and had a verbal confrontation with Richards, calling him a liar.

Sheriff David Anderson

Richards told Gemge that the next man that called him a liar would die. Gemge then put his hand on his "six shooter," but didn't realize the seriousness of his bluff. Richards pulled his pistol and shot and killed Gemge. Richards then gathered up his belongings and rode off, taking Gemge's horse with him. As he made his way towards Kearney, he ran across a settler and asked the man to tend to Gemge's horse, saying his partner would get it later. He then rode off towards town, leaving the settler with a new horse.[51]

Richards decided to stay in Kearney, and told his friends and new acquaintances he just returned from Colorado. Richards and his not so law abiding associates had one thing in common. They lived hard and enjoyed drinking, gambling, and consorting with what Richards referred to as "sporting women."[52]

Eventually Richards ran afoul of the law, and he and another man were arrested for murder and sent to the Buffalo County jail. Ironically, it was one of the murders in the area that Richards didn't commit, and he was able to establish an alibi and was subsequently released. During his stay, however, he rekindled his friendship with Mrs. Harelson, who also happened to be in jail at the time. She was suspected as being complicit in her husband's escape. It was in jail that Mrs. Harelson made the terrible mistake of inviting Richards to visit her at their farm when she was released.[53]

The Harelson's farm was located approximately 25 miles south of Kearney near Walker's Ranch.[54] After her husband fled Nebraska, Mrs. Harelson was left to care for the farm and her children. Daisy, her 10 year old daughter, was the oldest, Mabel, her 4 year old, was the middle child, and Jesse, her 2 year old toddler, was the youngest.[55]

Sometime during the first part of June, 1878, Richards went to the Harelson place. At first he helped with the chores, but soon got bored and asked for more. Mrs. Harelson agreed to sell Richards a quarter section of their land and provide a deed for him, but there would be a delay. It would be another six months before she could "prove up" their homestead and take title. Richards agreed to the deal, and decided to do some additional traveling until the land was available. Sometime during the first part of July of 1878, he ended up in Hastings, Nebraska and became familiar enough there to later say it was his "headquarters." He stayed there until the first part of October, when he went back to the Harelson farm. He planned on living there and working until he was able to close the land transaction.[56] He lasted about a month. By the first of November, 1878, Richards had made up his mind to kill Mrs. Harelson and her three children.[57]

The historical record of the murders of Mrs. Harelson and her children is somewhat clouded by the fact that Samuel D. Richards gave several interviews describing the gruesome act, and each time he retold the story, the facts were slightly altered in what appears to be an attempt to mitigate his deed.[58] The reality, however, is that when Richard's accounts are matched with the reports of those who discovered the bodies, nothing Richards said could have diluted his horrific crime.

Richards waited until all of his potential victims were asleep in their two room sod house. He went outside and dug a large trench to be used as a common grave, and quietly walked back into the house and over to the bed where Mrs. Harelson was soundly sleeping with her two girls. Using what was described as a large flat piece of iron, he struck Mrs. Harelson in the head with the sharp edge of the weapon. Her skull was crushed, and the coup de grace inflicted by what the evidence disclosed was a second blow. Richards quickly repeated the bashing of Daisy, and then Mabel, who both were still sleeping, and mercifully unaware of the horror surrounding them. The slaughter awoke the toddler, Jesse, and he began crying. Richards made quick work of him by grabbing him by the ankle and, using a whip like motion, bashed his head against the floor.[59]

Richards then carried the woman's body to the previously excavated grave. It was located behind a large haystack and described as "20 rods north of the house." Next, he carried the children's bodies, and placed them next to their mother. After all four bodies where in the grave, Richards covered them with dirt and hay.[60]

For several days, Richards continued to live on the property as though nothing had happened. When neighbors asked about the mother and children, Richards simply said that they had gone east to visit relatives. Richards traveled to Hastings and, after spending a few days there, came back to the farm, pretending as though the family would return after their trip.[61]

The motive for the killings were at first speculative. News reports said it was greed that drove Richards to do it, noting that he wanted all of the Harelson property for himself.[62] In what seems was the most candid confession, Richards said he killed her because she 'talked too much," asked too many questions, and had found out about his previous murders. He decided to kill her to keep her quiet, and had to kill the children too.[63]

About six miles east of the Harelson farm, a 26 year old immigrant from Sweden named Peter Anderson had established a small homestead. Anderson was a bachelor and spent most of his time building up his farm. Around December 1, 1878, Richards decided to pay Anderson a visit, and asked if he needed help with the chores.[64] Anderson agreed to hire Richards, and asked if had an ability to cook as well as tend to the other farm tasks. Richards gladly accepted the position, including the extra duty as a cook. On the 9th of December, Richards went out into the farm yard out of the sight of Anderson and dug another grave.[65]

After he finished digging the grave, Richards went into Anderson's house, and told him that he was in for a special surprise. Richards said he was going to prepare an extraordinary supper for him, and he was sure that he would thoroughly enjoy it.[66] Shortly after finishing his meal, Anderson began feeling ill. He went to the home of Godfrey Boostrom, a neighbor. Anderson's "tongue was swollen and he had definite symptoms of having been poisoned."[67] Anderson was sure that Richards had poisoned him, and mentioned that the two men had not been getting along. Boostrom and another neighbor, A. G. Anderson, no relation, provided Anderson with an antidote. They then urged him to stay away from his farm, noting that it may be dangerous to go back.[68]

Peter Anderson, unfortunately, did not heed their advice and returned to his farmstead. He immediately confronted Richards and accused him of the poisoning and trying to murder him. Richards decided that his newly acquired subtle approach to murder was not working for him. He picked up a hammer and smashed Anderson's skull. For some unknown reason, he also decided to abandon the idea of planting Anderson's body in the new grave he recently prepared. Instead, he drug Anderson's body down into the cellar, dug a shallow grave, and covered him in coal.[69]

Richards decided it was probably a good idea to move on, so he went out to the barn and began hitching up Anderson's team. The neighbor, A. G. Anderson, showed up to check on his friend Pete, and found Richards hooking up the team. He asked Richards where Peter was and if he was alright, to which Richards replied, "why don't you go inside and ask him."[70] A. G. Anderson went inside to make sure that Peter was safe, and while he was headed for the house, Richards pulled the harness off of one of the horses and rode off. Soon, a group of neighbors were at the farm searching for Peter, and when they found the empty fresh grave, they intensified their search. They quickly found Anderson in the cellar.[71]

As soon as the neighbors realized that Richards had killed Anderson and fled, the buzz turned to the absent Harelson family. The neighbors decided to travel to the farm, and became wary when they entered the home and found the family's clothes still there. With that discovery, they became suspicious and feared the worst. They began searching the farm, and found the horror under the haystack.[72]

Sheriff Matthew Kieran was the Kearney County Sheriff at the time of the murders, and because the crimes occurred within his jurisdiction, he was the first lawman trying to find Richards. The town of Kearney, in Buffalo County, was the jurisdiction of Sheriff David Anderson. Anderson, sometimes called "Cap," was a civil war veteran and known as an aggressive, no nonsense sheriff. After getting the news of the crimes, he quickly became involved in the pursuit. Sheriff S. Lewis Martin from Hastings, which is located in Adams County, also played a significant role in the search for Richards. Richards' flight first took him to Red Cloud, and then to Hastings, his old "headquarters." In Hastings he was able to catch a train that would take him back to his home in Ohio.[73]

Sheriff Anderson was first to find out that Richards had left Hastings by train, and sent a telegram to John H Butler, Omaha's chief of police. Anderson's wire notified Butler that Richards was probably headed east, and was wanted for murdering five people in Kearney County. Butler and several of his policemen hurried to Omaha's Union Station and met the train from Hastings. Richards slipped the dragnet, however, because Butler intercepted the Union Pacific train and was not aware that the Burlington and Missouri River line also had an eastbound train from Hastings. Richards was on the other train.[74] Governor Silas Garber authorized a reward of $200 for the capture of Richards, "Dead or Alive."[75]

"If I'd had my shootin' irons along I'd never been taken," is what he told a reporter from the *Chicago Inter Ocean News*.[76] Richards was apprehended in Steubenville, Ohio on December 15, 1878. He was recognized by a man who was a boyhood acquaintance. The man was working as a guard at the Ohio Penitentiary and happened to spot Richards as he was escorting two women home from a dance. The guard was aware of Richards' crimes in Nebraska and knew he was a wanted man. He notified a constable and they both arrested Richards as he walked through a field. The penitentiary guard eventually claimed and got the reward.[77]

After hearing that Richards slipped Chief Butler's trap in Omaha, Sheriff Anderson headed for Chicago. He was soon followed by Sheriff Martin, who was also anxious to get his hands on Richards. Shortly after the two lawmen began their search for the escapee, they were notified that Richards had been apprehended in Steubenville.[78]

On December 28, 1878, the two Sheriffs had taken care of the appropriate extradition paperwork and were quickly on the Burlington train back to Omaha with Richards in tow. When they arrived at Omaha, they switched trains to the Union Pacific, and headed towards Kearney and the Buffalo County jail. A crowd of 200 gathered at the station in Kearney in anticipation of Richard's return, but Sheriff Anderson got word and sent a message for deputies to meet the train a few miles east of Kearney. When the two Sheriffs stepped off of the train empty handed, the disappointed crowd was told by Sheriff Anderson that they left Richards in the Hall County jail in Grand Island, fearing that

Richards would be lynched if they brought him to Kearney. The plan worked, and Richards would live to stand trial.[79]

On Wednesday January 15, 1879, Samuel D Richards, (also known as Stephen) went on trial for the murder of Peter Anderson at Minden, Nebraska. Since Sheriff Matthew Kieran had no jail in Kearney County, Richards was housed at the Buffalo County jail located in the town of Kearney. He was transported approximately 20 miles to the courthouse at Minden for the proceedings.[80]

The prosecutor in the case was District Attorney Thomas D. Scofield, and Samuel L. Savidge of Kearney was appointed by the court to defend Richards. Judge William Gaslin presided over the trial. Mr. Scofield began the trial by first reading the indictment. Richards pled not guilty.[81] The State called only three witnesses; C Lawson, A.G. Anderson, and Mr. Hubbard, before Judge Gaslin said the State had clearly established their case and refused Scofield's request to allow more witnesses. Mr. Savidge then put Richards on the stand. He testified that he had killed Anderson in self-defense only after he was attacked. He also denied poisoning Anderson, and called A. G. Anderson a liar.[82]

The closing arguments were very brief as was Judge Gaslin's charge to foreman Samuel Beebe and the rest of the jury. Gaslin told the jury they could convict for first degree murder, second degree murder, or acquit Richards.[83]

The jury was out approximately an hour. They voted several times, but were stalemated at six for first degree and six for second degree. When they reported back to the Judge, he became angry and told the Sheriff to take the jury back to deliberate again, and not to come back without a unanimous decision. They were out for over another hour, and finally returned a verdict of guilty in the first degree.[84]

As soon as the jury was excused, Judge Gaslin asked Richards if he had anything to say before the Court passed sentence upon him. Richards replied that he had nothing to say, and Gaslin quickly pronounced the sentence. "It is thereupon considered and adjudged by the court, that you, Stephen D Richards, be confined in the jail of Kearney County, Nebraska until Saturday, April 26, 1879, and it is further considered and adjudged by the court that on the 26th day of April, 1879, between the hours of 10:00 AM and 4:00 PM of said day, you'd be hanged by the neck until you are dead."[85]

A prudent Sheriff Anderson, in consultation with Sheriff Kieran, reckoned if they kept Richards in the Buffalo County jail, he would not make it until April. They were sure he would be the guest of honor at a necktie party. The two men worked out an agreement with Warden H. C. Dawson to house him in the penitentiary at Lincoln for safekeeping. He was housed at the prison until the night before his execution.[86]

Because the Statute mandated the sheriff of the county in which the capital crime was committed was in charge of implementing all phases of the process, Sheriff Kieran went to work and made sure that all of the preparations for the hanging were in place. The law also provided that the hanging was to be in the "immediate vicinity" of the jail in the county in which the crime was committed, and an enclosure was to be erected around the gallows to shield the event from the public.[87]

The Sheriff had the enclosure built and also made arrangements for extra deputies to guard against an intrusion by the public. He even went to the trouble of having special admittance passes printed. In addition, he spent $80.00 on the gallows, $10.00 on a coffin for Richards, and paid $2.00 each to Anthony Stokes and George Van Ski to dig a grave.[88]

On the morning of the 25 of April, 1879, Sheriff Kieran, in the company of Kearney District Court Clerk L. A. Hunt and Lancaster County Sheriff J. S. Hoagland, arrived at the penitentiary in Lincoln to pick up Richards. Richards was placed in irons and turned over to the Sheriff, but not before the State's physician gave Richards 3 tablespoons of brandy to calm his nerves. Sheriff Kieran and Mr. Hunt escorted the shackled Richards to a waiting carriage at the steps to the prison. They were followed by Sheriff Hoagland and Warden Dawson. The entire entourage boarded the carriage and set out for the train depot. The station was crowded with curious onlookers trying to get a glimpse of Richards. The group had to push their way through the crowd in order to board the train, but in the end they were all treated to a look, and also got a bonus in the form of a speech from Richards. He only said a few words, and ended with, "I bid you all goodbye."[89]

Sheriff Kieran and Mr. Hunt took Richards directly to the Kearney County Sheriff's office at the courthouse in Minden, where he was placed under guard by four additional deputy sheriffs and the Minden constable. Richards was awake all night and snacked on "peaches and crackers." He was kept busy signing his autographs and talking to reporters. At 4:00 A.M., Dr. Vandenberg checked his wellbeing and noted that his pulse was beating at 75 beats per minute and normal. At 8:00, he re-checked Richards and found him still not having anxiety

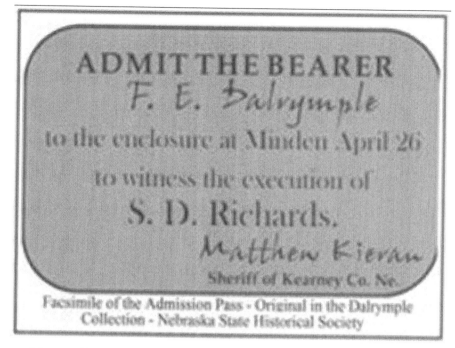

ADMIT THE BEARER

F. E. Dalrymple

to the enclosure at Minden April 26

to witness the execution of

S. D. Richards,

Matthew Kieran

Sheriff of Kearney Co. Ne.

Facsimile of the Admission Pass - Original in the Dalrymple
Collection - Nebraska State Historical Society

problems. He noted his heart rate had actually slowed to 65 beats per minute. During the rest of the morning, Richards spent time with Chaplin Gee, his spiritual adviser, and continued to talk to reporters.[90] While Richards was preparing to meet his doom, Sheriff Kieran was dealing with another problem.

The crowd of onlookers grew to what was later estimated to be at least 1,500 people. The Sheriff had placed a rope around the outside of the barricade to keep back the masses.[91] The *Omaha Daily Republican* described the crowd by saying, "If it had been the Fourth of July, the interest manifested could not have been greater. Fathers mother and children and one or two babies at the breast were sickening evidence of the wish to see the last moments of Richards."[92]

Sometime around noon, the spectators grew restless and tired of being restrained by a rope. A few of the men began cutting the rope, and after several attempts at repairing it failed, the guards simply disregarded the barrier.[93] It wasn't long before others began working on the boards comprising the stockade wall, which hid the yard and the gallows. As soon as a few parts of the barricade were torn down, the crowd, en masse, would cheer, and then a few more pieces would go down until only about one half of it was standing. The Sheriff and his deputies were able to move back the crowd, but just momentarily.[94]

At 12:44 P.M., the crowd grew still as a horse drawn carriage slowly made its way to the gallows. Deputy Sheriff Peters drove the rig with Mr. Gee next to him facing back, looking at an unshackled Richards, who was in the back seat with Sheriff Kieran. Mr. Hunt was also in the carriage, while Dawson County Sheriff James walked along side. The crowd went from a quiet drone to a complete hush as Richards climbed the steps to the scaffold.[95]

Sheriff Kieran read the death warrant out loud in a strong voice while Richards stood silently looking out at the crowd. It was 12:58 P.M. when he finished, and he immediately began tying Richard's hands, then his thighs, and finally his ankles. Richards was given an opportunity to address the crowd, and simply said that he had made his peace with God and said farewell to several people and the crowd in general. Reverend Gee then stepped forward and read selected verses from the Bible. Gee then knelt down and prayed for Richards. Richards then said, "I die for the crimes they say I have committed. Jesus be with me now." At 1:07, Sheriff Kieran placed the noose around Richards' neck and adjusted it. Next he placed the black cap over Richards' head, and the Sheriff, without hesitation, stepped back and kicked the support holding the trap secure, allowing Richards to fall.[96]

"The scaffold creaked and a look of horror passed over the crowd with many turning their heads."[97] The sound was described as a "dull but very loud thud."[98] Richards fell at least 5 feet, and his body contorted several times as though "he was trying to breathe."[99]

Dr. J. Albert Vandenberg and Dr. F. E. Dalrymple were the attending physicians. The first check of his pulse took place at exactly 1:16, about a minute after Richards dropped through the trap door. Richards' pulse was 100. At 1:23, the doctors reported that the pulse was too fast to count, and finally, at 1:51, Richards was pronounced dead. Richards' body was cut down and placed in a coffin to be taken to the Minden Cemetery for burial. Drs. Vandenberg and Dalrymple had previously asked that they be allowed to conduct an autopsy, but were denied.[100] Scientists of the period were convinced that criminals like Richards had an underlying physiological problem that caused their behavior, and Drs. Vandenberg and Dalrymple wanted to have a look.[101]

Within two days, the body of Samuel D. Richards had been unearthed, despite the efforts of the Sheriff to protect the gravesite. The stories of what exactly happened to the remains are varied. It seems to be a fact that an autopsy was performed, which left little doubt who was responsible for the grave robbery. People reported seeing some of Richards' body parts spread over the town. The conjecture was that they had been discarded, and the town's feral dogs took them from a refuse pile as a prize.[102] Other reports were that Dr. Dalrymple "whitened the bones" and displayed the skeleton at his office. Richards' skull, however, purportedly ended up on display in the front window of the *Kearney County Gazette*.[103] The citizens of Kearney County were satisfied that Richards would never kill again.

Chapter II
Orlando Casler
Union Soldier

In the spring of 1879, specifically in the months of April and May, five people were scheduled to hang for murder in Nebraska.[104] That seems like a high number of slated executions for any State, particularly in 1879. It's important to consider that Nebraska's population back then only numbered 120,000 people, while Iowa, for example, Nebraska's neighbor to the east, had nearly 1,200,000 or ten times as many people within the State.[105] The high number of executions is really not too surprising when you consider a couple of factors. First, arguments in the new frontier were often settled by one person simply pulling out a pistol and shooting the other, and second, Nebraska in 1878 was still unsettled and considered part of the Wild West.[106] Although the static population was small, the transitory numbers were high as people migrated west.

How prevalent was homicide in Nebraska back then? During a 10 day stretch in December of 1878, "thirteen or fourteen" murders were committed within the State.[107] After S. D. Richards' trial, Judge Gaslin commented, "Since 1873, I can call to mind twelve persons that have been murdered in this county, and only one man has been brought to justice therefor." The Judge then commented on the rash of recent murders in his judicial district by saying "within six weeks, I have disposed of twenty-six murder cases."[108]

How many of those pioneer killers were apprehended and paid the ultimate price for their deed? The answer is that some were lynched or legally hung, but not all of them. Besides S. D. Richards, who met the hangman that April in 1879, a doctor named George St. Louis was sentenced to hang for killing his wife in Fremont, Nebraska; H. C. Schlencker was sentenced for killing his mistress in Lincoln; J. McElvoy was sentenced for killing Henry Stutzman near Hastings; and Orlando Casler was scheduled to die for killing George Munroe at Seward, Nebraska.[109]

Dr. St. Louis cheated the hangman by shooting himself in his jail cell the day before his scheduled execution; H. C. Schlencker made two trips to the Nebraska Supreme Court and ended up with a life sentence and a subsequent pardon; J. McElvoy appealed his case to the Nebraska Supreme Court, and when it was remanded for a new trial, he pled guilty and got a life sentence. Orlando Casler, on the other hand, was not as lucky as the others. He couldn't escape the rope.[110]

Casler was also known as Orlando Cassler, and like many persons of the day, seemed to take a good deal of liberty when it came to spelling his surname. The name was thought to be Americanized from the German spelling, Kesler.[111] Orlando Casler served in the Union Army during the Civil War and was attached to the 16th Regiment New York Heavy Artillery. He enlisted on December 21, 1863, and was discharged "for disability" on May 25, 1865, under the name of Orlando Cassler.[112]

Orlando was born on January 28, 1847 in Herkimer County, New York. According to John Waterman, author of General History of Seward County, Nebraska, Orlando Casler was a criminaloid (criminal) whose father served a stretch in the New York Penitentiary on a charge of manslaughter.[113] Casler was one of seven children. He had five brothers and one sister. Casler's disability was the result of taking a Confederate ball in his left shoulder during the Civil War. One of his brothers was killed in the War, another died in California, and yet another in New York. His sister, Lany, her husband, T. H. Tisdale, and another brother left New York and homesteaded in Seward County, Nebraska, while the remaining brother moved to Wisconsin.[114]

Shortly after the War, Orlando traveled to Winona, Wisconsin to visit his brother. Eventually, he was married in Wisconsin, and tried settling down and raising a family. According to Orlando, he was picked up one day by a man named Henry Hardy, who just happened to be driving a team of stolen horses.[115] Subsequently, on May 11, 1870, Casler was sentenced to the Wisconsin State prison for 5 years from Dodge County, Wisconsin for his alleged participation in the theft. On September 12, 1872, Orlando was given a pardon. The prosecuting attorney asked the Governor to pardon Orlando, citing "good conduct in prison and great doubt as to his guilt."[116]

In May of 1874, Orlando had enough of Wisconsin, so with his wife and their 5 children set out for Seward County, Nebraska. His intent was to establish a homestead and make a living farming. At first, Casler lived with his brother and sister near

Beaver Crossing, but eventually Casler was able to move into a "dug-out" that belonged to a benevolent bachelor named White.[117] White got impatient and decided to vacate his homestead and relinquish his claim before his "prove up" was complete to a man named Salnave. Salnave paid White a small amount of cash for this consideration. Casler became aware of White's move and the transaction with Salnave and went to the land office and filed his own homestead claim before Salnave, cheating him out of the land.[118] John Waterman, author of <u>General History of Seward County, Nebraska</u>, was a neighbor of Casler and well acquainted with him. Waterman said that Casler was much better off than many of those who were homesteading the area, primarily because he received a disability pension from the Army. Waterman added that Casler brought a "mania" for horses with him from Wisconsin.[119]

In June of 1878, George L. Munroe left his home in Arkansas City, Missouri and headed out driving a covered wagon and a team of horses. He came to Nebraska and bought some land in Saunders County. On July 6, 1878, quite by accident, he stumbled upon Orlando Casler as he happened to be traveling in Seward County near the area of Beaver Crossing.[120] As the two men talked, they seemed to recognize each other, and realized they had met during the Civil War. As they talked and shared their experiences, the conversation became friendlier. Casler eventually extended an invitation to Munroe and asked him to spend some time at the Casler farm. Munroe accepted Orlando's hospitality and stayed with the Casler and his family for about three days.[121]

Orlando or "Lant," as his wife and friends called him, asked Munroe to sell him his team of horses. They agreed on a price of $250.00, and Casler gave Munroe a $100.00 down payment. Casler and Munroe arranged to travel to the town of Seward in order for Casler to get the rest of the money.[122]

On Sunday July 7, 1878, the two hitched up the team and set off for Seward, traveling nearly twenty miles before stopping. Just before they reached Seward, they decided to pitch camp next to the Blue River, which is situated just to the southwest of the town. When the camp was settled, they went into Seward, bought some provisions for supper, and then traveled back to their camp.[123] Upon returning, the two men found that a party of four other men had also made camp just a short distance from theirs. Casler and Munroe broke their camp and moved further up the river, where they prepared another camp site. According to witnesses, Casler was overheard as saying that the men were moving because the mosquitoes were a problem, and he was sure they would not be as bothersome up river.[124]

According to Casler, it rained during the night and the two were forced to sleep under the wagon. He said when they awoke, they found that the horses had gotten loose during the night, and they were forced to round them up. After they caught and harnessed the horses, they ate breakfast and headed for Seward, where they concluded all of their business. Casler then headed home with his new team and wagon, while Munroe set out for California.[125]

What really happened at the campsite is, as they say, a horse of a different color. On Thursday, three days after they broke camp, a man by the name of Cowden and his 6 year old son were fishing on the Blue River below where Munroe and Casler were camped. The boy told the father that there was a man on the other side of the river in the water. At first, Mr. Cowden ignored the boy, but the lad's insistence forced Cowden to look, and sure enough he saw not a man, but a body of a man in the river bobbing up and down behind a log. The County Coroner, Mr. Woodward, was notified immediately, and began looking into the matter. It was quickly determined that the body was George L. Munroe based upon several items found on the body, including a diary and a letter from Munroe's wife dated June 23, 1878. Munroe's wife signed the letter "From Lizzy, write as often as you can." In her letter, she told George that she had not as yet sold their farm, and she lamented over how bad the times were. George was apparently on a mission to find a better life for the couple.[126]

A post mortem exam determined that Munroe died from a gunshot wound through his heart. When the coroner looked further he also found a severe gash on the side of Munroe's head. He speculated that Munroe was first struck with the gun butt, causing the hammer to put the gash on his head, and then Munroe was fatally shot.[127] There was no question, in the mind of Woodward, that George Munroe was murdered.[128]

About 3 A.M. the next morning, Casler's neighbor, John Waterman, was awakened by a pounding on the door of his dug-out. When he answered, it was Seward County Sheriff John Sullivan, who said there had been a murder, and he and some of his neighbors were being summoned to a coroner's jury in Seward. Sheriff Sullivan rounded up several people from the area, and soon he and his deputy followed a parade of wagons into Seward. The sheriff, it was later determined, made sure that

Orlando was included in his jury muster, and that he stayed behind, not in front, of Casler's wagon.[129]

At Seward, on the 11th of July, 1878, Coroner Woodward conducted a coroner's inquest into Munroe's death. Several witnesses testified concerning the activities of the two men both before and after they reached Seward. Other witnesses were called, including the campers that intruded into the original campsite. They testified that when they awoke on the morning of the 8th, they observed Orlando trying to grab the loose horses. They each said that they helped capture them, but swore that when they tried to drive them back to Casler's camp, he was adamant about not letting them into the campsite. The men also asked about the other man, meaning Munroe, and were told by Casler that he had "taken sick" and had "gone up town to get something for his relief."[130] One important fact brought out that seemed to establish intent was that Orlando did not actually have the money or assets to purchase the horses and wagon from Munroe.

The inquest continued until the 15th of July, 1878, at which time the coroner's jury of six men and Coroner J. H. Woodward issued its verdict. The jurors concluded that George L. Munroe died at the hands of Orlando Casler, who "unlawfully, feloniously, willfully and of his deliberate and his premeditated malice, did kill and murder Munroe".[131]

In November of 1878, a grand jury was convened to re-hear the evidence against Casler. Twelve jurors and the foreman, Marshall J. Houck, had to determine if the evidence was strong enough to bring Casler to trial. On November 4, 1878, the grand jury returned an indictment of murder against Orlando Casler.[132]

The trial of Orlando Casler began on January 28, 1879 before Judge George W. Post. The case for the prosecution was presented by Manoah Reese, who would later become a Nebraska Supreme Court Judge. The trial lasted an entire week, mainly because the State brought 28 witnesses to testify against Orlando.[133] The evidence against Casler was all circumstantial, but there was plenty of it and it was strong. Several people saw Casler in Seward on the Monday morning after the murder, and they all testified that his clothing was wet. The inference made by the prosecution was that he not only dumped Munroe's body, but that he had tried to weight it down. When Sheriff Sullivan and his men searched Casler's stable, they found Munroe's pistol, which someone had gone to the trouble of hiding. They also searched Casler's house and found Munroe's pocketbook and personal papers hidden in Orlando's bed. A suitcase containing Munroe's clothing was found hidden beside the road which led back to Beaver Crossing from Seward. In addition, apparently, Orlando shared the details of the crime with his wife, who told some of the other neighbors.[134] The only evidence for the defense was Orlando's testimony and several neighbors who testified as character witnesses. Casler took the stand and retold his version of the incidents, and insisted that when he parted company with Munroe that he was alive and in good spirits.[135] On February 4, 1879, Judge Post charged the jury and provided them with instructions. It took the jury just 1 hour and 20 minutes to reach a verdict of guilty of murder in the first-degree.[136] Two days later, Orlando appeared before Judge Post to hear his sentence. The Judge pronounced that Casler be hanged on May 20, 1879, "by the neck until you are dead."[137]

As Sheriff John Sullivan began preparations for hanging Orlando Casler, he faced the same task as his counterpart, Kearney County Sheriff Kieran. He had to build a scaffold and ensure that an adequate enclosure was built enclosing the gallows from public view. He also considered the option of issuing passes or credentials to those who by law could be admitted to the spectacle.[138] Everything was progressing smoothly for Sheriff Sullivan, but that was before the execution in Kearney County. After the problems encountered by Sheriff Kieran in Minden, Sheriff Sullivan began scrambling to try and figure out a way to avoid a similar scene in Seward.

Sheriff Sullivan sensed that the bloodlust attitude in Minden would not be any less for those who planned on coming to see Casler hung. A week before the execution, on May 15, 1879, he sent a letter to Nebraska Governor Albinus Nance and hinted that he wouldn't be opposed if the Governor sent in the militia to keep the stockade intact and the execution from being made public. The governor quickly sent back a caustic response that, in essence, told Sheriff Sullivan that he was in-charge of the hanging and he should do his job and keep the peace. The last line of the governor's response was, in a chastising tone, "show to the people of Nebraska that the curiosity of mobs cannot be satisfied at the expense of law and order." [139] Sheriff Sullivan was determined to do the best he could with a situation that he knew was going to be difficult.[140] The sheriff knew that his problem would be more difficult than Sheriff Kieran's, simply based on the higher number of people in Seward County.

The population of Kearney County in 1878 was 1,517, while Seward County had 7,991 people.[141] The population of the town of Seward, the county seat and the place where Casler was to hang, was 1,525.[142] By the early morning hours of May 20, 1879, the town of Seward had grown by an estimated 3,000 people.[143] By 12:30, news reports placed the number of people gathered at the courthouse to be between 5,000 and 8,000 people.[144] Reporters covering the hanging also noted in their reports that the gathering reminded them of the incident at Minden the month before.[145] The first to go was a wire fence around the perimeter of the wooden privacy stockade. Next, the crowd began tearing off the boards, one-by-one, until the entire wall was down and the gallows exposed. The destruction was completed in less than 3 minutes. Sheriff Sullivan climbed the steps onto the scaffold and addressed the crowd. He told them that it was just past 12:30, and Casler was to be hung between 1 P.M. and 4 P.M. He also said that the hanging would take place as scheduled, provided that the crowd back up a reasonable distance from the gallows. The crowd seemed satisfied and backed away.[146]

At 1:15 P.M., Casler's spiritual adviser, the Reverend J. W. Shank, and another minister, each held one of Casler's arms as they walked him to the steps of the gallows. Casler mounted the stairs with a "firm and steady step," and stood erect awaiting the proceedings.[147] Sheriff Sullivan and his deputy were already on the scaffold, along with Lancaster County Sheriff J. S. Hoagland and County Clerk Graham.[148]

Mr. Graham stepped forward and read the death warrant, including the instructions from Judge Post. Next, Casler was allowed to speak, and despite the overwhelming circumstantial evidence, protested the hanging and declared his innocence. The Reverend Shanks then read selections from the Bible and offered several prayers. Casler then spoke up and asked that the crowd be allowed to sing a hymn. The once raucous, bloodthirsty crowd, which was now subdued by the solemnness of the situation, joined in and belted out the song, "Oh what a friend we have in Jesus." At the conclusion of the hymn, Casler once again addressed the crowd. He spoke in the third person saying, "Well I expect this will finish Orlando Casler," and finished by saying, "Goodbye to you all."[149] As soon as Casler finished speaking, Sheriff Sullivan stepped up and asked Casler if he had a confession to make. Casler said, once more, that he was innocent. The sheriff stood patiently while Casler was quickly bound, and then he put a black hood over his head and adjusted the noose on his neck.[150]

At 1:29 P.M., Sheriff Sullivan released the trap door, and Orlando Casler dropped five feet to his death. Reporters noted that his neck was broken and all of his vital functions stopped 9 minutes after the trap door was sprung.[151] According to the sheriffs' notes on his return of the death warrant, Drs. Arvin Beechley and William Hastings were in attendance.[152] Orlando Casler was buried in the cemetery at Beaver Crossing, Nebraska, but as far as being "the finish," as Casler predicted, it was not.

In 1929, William H. Smith, editor of the *Seward Independent-Democrat, launched a movement to mark Casler's grave with the distinction of being a Civil War veteran.* His editorial said, "He (Casler) had served his country with honor in its time of trial." It was 50 years after the execution, and Smith said it was time to honor the veteran, and not dishonor the man because he was a murderer. Today, decorating Casler's grave is the traditional Grand Army of the Republic plaque, "GAR 1861-1865."[153]

Honorable Manoah Reese

Casler verdict

Judge William Gaslin - 1868
Courtesy - Nebraska State Historical Society

Judge Post judgment sentence

Sheriff Sullivan return

Chapter III
Milton Wisdom Smith
A May-December Romance

An editorial in the *Osceola Record* said that, "No more heartless or cold blooded murder was ever committed in the history of Nebraska, nor one with less provocation."[154] The editorial was referring to the 1884 case of Milton W. Smith of Osceola, Nebraska. The editorial staff of the *Omaha Daily Bee* also commented on the case by saying, "The murder committed by Smith was one of the most cold-blooded deeds imaginable."[155] Were the editors of these early journals overstating the appalling nature of what Smith did? At that time and place, probably not, but to better answer the question, it's necessary to look at what the paper referred to as Smith's "deeds."

Milton Smith and Ruth M. McMurphy were married in Cass, Illinois in 1856. After their marriage, the couple moved from place to place in Illinois, but after a few years they relocated to Iowa and settled in the southeastern part in Jefferson County. At the time, Milton listed his occupation as a farmer, but also worked occasionally as a carpenter.[156]

Ruth was Milton's second wife. It is believed that his first wife, Sarah, passed away in Dewitt County, Illinois not long after they were married.[157] Eventually, in 1873, Milton, Ruth, and their 9 children moved to Osceola in Nebraska, where they planned on establishing a homestead.[158] Milton was 46 years old and Ruth 11 years his junior at 35 at the time of the move. Between 1873 and 1884, Ruth gave birth to 4 more children, George, Alice, Lucy, and Thomas, which brought the number of their offspring to 13.[159] The couple maintained their farm for a few years, but it eventually failed. The loss was primarily due to the fact that Milton drank too much and was not a good provider. They eventually moved to a house in Osceola. Milton developed a reputation around town for being a ne're-do-well and a drunk. Ruth, unlike her husband, was well liked and respected in the community.[160] Ruth was forced to take in washing in order to support the family, and for years, they barely eked out a living.[161]

Marital problems were commonplace between Ruth and her husband. She blamed Milton's drinking, and was sure it was the alcohol that caused the constant bickering. Often the quarrels escalated to violence, and eventually Milton began beating Ruth on a regular basis. His constant abusive behavior was the norm, and he didn't give it a second thought. Ruth, however, who at first was fearful, became terrified of him. The cycle continued for years. First the confrontation, followed by a beating, then the insincere apology, and then a reconciliation.[162]

In 1876, Milton was accused of molesting his 11 year old daughter. He was subsequently arrested and charged with incest.[163] His case went through the court system, but in the end, there wasn't enough evidence to convict him.[164] Ruth could do little and was forced to endure the situation for several more years. On June 6, 1884, however, an incident occurred that caused a chain reaction that sent things spiraling out of control.

Milton came home drunk, and as usual, the couple began to argue. The argument quickly escalated, and in a violent rage, Milton, "beat Ruth with a piece of wood."[165] She, along with the children, was forced from the home. It was the middle of the night, and they had nowhere to go. Ruth and the children were forced to spend the night sleeping on the ground without the benefit of pillows, blankets, or any other comforts.[166] At that point, Ruth decided she had finally had enough and filed a peace bond against Milton. In effect, because of Nebraska law, Milton was required to put up a bond that ensured he would stay away from Ruth and the children. For some reason, the bondsman decided to revoke the bond after a few days, which sent Milton directly to the Polk County jail.[167]

The judge eventually was convinced that Smith would leave the jurisdiction if he was released. He decided that may be the best way to solve his problem and struck out to find work in Long Pine, Nebraska, which is an area about 200 miles north and west of Osceola. Smith was told that he could find work there.

On July 15, 1884, J. L. Walkeevor, an attorney retained by Ruth, filed a petition for divorce on her behalf. The plea asked the court to grant a divorce to the petitioner on the grounds of "Extreme Cruelty."[168] The attorney detailed the case, noting the regular beatings to which Ruth was subjected over the years.

Meanwhile, Milton worked on and off as a carpenter at Long Pine for 3 months before deciding that it was probably safe to go back to Osceola.[169] The divorce case was scheduled for the fall term of the court, and Milton wanted to be back in Osceola when it was heard. He arrived back sometime in October, the specific dates are not known.[170] During the latter part of October and through November, Milton kept busy working at several carpenter jobs around Osceola.[171] On Thanksgiving Day, November 27, 1884, Ruth saw Milton loitering near the house, and became frightened. She decided to take action and got word to the court that she was in fear of Milton. Her attorney, Mr. Walkeevor, asked the court for a "peace bond," which in effect was a restraining order keeping Milton away from his farm and Ruth.[172] When Milton found out what Ruth had done, he became irate.[173]

Later, he would say that he was not loitering near the home, but was there with a considerate purpose. He said there was no reason why Ruth should have felt distressed. He explained that he had purchased a suit of clothes for their son George, who was then 7 years old, and simply wanted to show Ruth that he was providing for the boy. He also said he hoped that she would let him visit and see their three other children, 8 year old Lucy, 4 year old Alice, and baby Tommy, who was 17 months old.[174]

Milton spent the day drinking, and became more irritated as the day turned into later afternoon. Meanwhile, Ruth was at home routinely taking care of the children winding down from a busy Thanksgiving Day. It was early evening when Milton's anger overtook him. He went back to the home and softly walked up to the front door and very quietly opened it. The first thing he saw was Ruth sitting next to the stove, holding their youngest on her lap. According to reports, she was nursing, or "holding him at her breast." Her three younger children were also in the room. Milton stepped into the house and pointed a pistol at his estranged wife. The first round was a misfire, and the gun made what was described as a "snapping" sound. A startled Ruth reacted by jumping to her feet while still cradling her child in her arms. Milton's second shot hit Ruth in the side, causing severe damage to her torso.[175] The shot was described as being so loud that everyone in the house began screaming. Milton then panicked and ran out of the house.[176]

He quickly fled the scene, and tried to hide in a cornfield near the house. A group of neighborhood men began searching for Smith, and it wasn't long before they found him cowering in the dark. The men decided that it would be best served if Judge Lynch rather than the regular courts handled the case, but Polk county sheriff Lemuel D. Hamilton was able to save Milton from the mob. The Sheriff took Smith into custody and was able to get past the mob and move him to the County jail, which fortunately for

Smith, was not far from where he was captured.[177] The crowd remained outside of the jail while considering their next move from a list of options. Storming the jail and lynching him was on the top of the list, and it was also second, third, and fourth.

Meanwhile, Smith somehow got his hands on a razor and allegedly attempted suicide by cutting his throat. When the mob heard Smith took a razor to his neck, they assumed he was done for, and there was no longer a need for a necktie party. The sheriff, however, promptly got Smith medical attention, and he lived to face the charges. Later, there was speculation that Smith did not truly want to kill himself, but simply wanted to avoid being lynched.[178] Ruth lived only a few hours past midnight, and then succumbed to her injury. She died on Friday, November 28, 1884.[179]

On December 4, 1884, the coroner issued the actual warrant ensuring Smith would be confined in the Polk County jail until the spring session of the District Court.[180] Public sentiment concerning Smith's crime and failed suicide attempt did not diminish during Smith's jail stay. An editorial sent to the *Omaha Daily Bee* in Omaha on December 22, 1884, said that "the bloodthirsty Smith" was "kicking about the grub" furnished him in jail, and that "a little hemp mixed with a telegraph pole would cure all of his problems."[181]

Smith was forced to continue complaining about the bad "grub," while he waited for grand jury to be summoned. On March 18, 1885, Smith's case was presented to the grand jury by District Attorney Thomas Darnall. On Wednesday, March 18, 1884, Joseph Miller, who was the foreman of the grand jury, announced that they had found adequate evidence against Smith and indicted him for first degree murder.[182]

The following day, March 19, 1885, Smith appeared before District Judge T. L. Norval and was officially arraigned. Smith was asked for his plea, and he responded, "I suppose I must have killed her but it was not premeditated." Judge Norval entered a plea of not guilty on Smith's behalf. Based upon the severity of the crime and Smith's indigence, Judge Norval appointed Osceola attorneys M. A. Mills, a State Senator from Osceola, and R. Wheeler to help defend Smith. The Judge also assigned Attorney J. W. Edgerton from Stromsburg, Nebraska to the defense team. District Attorney Tom Darnall continued as the state's prosecutor with the help of another prominent attorney, Mr. E. L. King.[183]

The trial of Milton W. Smith began immediately after his arraignment. His defense attorneys moved for a change of venue, arguing that Smith could not get a fair trial in Osceola. Judge Norval wasted no time in rejecting the request and ordered the trial to begin.[184] The next problem encountered by court was seating an unbiased jury. The attorneys were unable to seat a jury from those that had been called for the regular panel, and Judge Norval sent for an additional 60 jurors "from remote parts of the county."[185] The jury was finally seated around 2 P.M. on the following day. A total of 144 men were eventually called and examined as potential jurors. Of the 144 called, 132 of them were rejected based upon the fact that they were unable to say that they could make an impartial decision.[186]

The state's first witnesses testified that Smith made several threats against his wife in the past. They also testified that he often menaced and threatened others as well. Next to testify were several persons in the house at the time of the actual shooting, including the couple's older children. The district attorney, Mr. Darnall, then called L. Gephard, I. D. Chamberlain, and Howard Eckert. They testified that they were part of the group that captured Smith right after the shooting. The state established the cause of death using the testimony of the attending physicians, Drs. Mills, Hayden, and Whaley.[187]

Milton's attorneys were faced with showing some mitigating circumstances in an attempt to lessen the degree of Smith's guilt. They considered using insanity saying he was unable to premeditate the murder, therefore; making the crime second degree. Dr. Matthewson from Nebraska's "insane hospital" was prepared to testify for the defense. There was a conference held between Matthewson and Drs. Mills, Hayden, and Whaley. The result of the session was that Dr. Matthewson was prepared to testify that Smith was insane, and the other three would testify that Smith was of sound mind when he shot Ruth. His attorneys decided against using the defense, and instead put Smith on the stand. He told the story again that he only wanted to see his children and did not go to the house intending to shoot Ruth.[188]

Judge Norval recessed the court on Sunday after three grueling days of trial and saved the closing arguments for Monday, March 23. The trial resumed on Monday with both sides arguing their case before the jury. Judge Norval meticulously gave the jury their charge, which included a total of 26 instructions. It took the jury just 40 minutes to reach a verdict. The jury reported they found Smith, "guilty of first degree murder as he stands charged in the indictment."[189] At 4:00 P.M., foreman C. W. Talbot reported that the jury also believed Smith should hang for his crime. Judge Norval concurred, and set the date of Smith's hanging on July 24, 1885.[190]

M. A. Hill immediately filed a motion on behalf of Smith to set aside the verdict, and asked for a new trial. Hill included in his argument that there was "insufficient evidence," and eight other reasons that Smith should have a new trial. Judge Norval ruled that Hill's arguments were without merit and denied his request.[191] Smith was then escorted back to the Polk county jail to await his fate.[192]

Smith spent the next few months in jail refusing to shave or have his hair cut. He cursed the people of Osceola and complained constantly about his situation, blaming everyone, especially Ruth. Prior to the incident, he continually complained to anyone who would listen that his wife was unfaithful. Those who knew the couple dismissed the charges, and considered that it was all a product of Milton's imagination.[193]

About a week prior to the hanging, Deputy United States Marshal R. E. Allan, from Omaha, stopped to see Smith at the Polk County jail. Allen was acquainted with Smith in Jefferson County, Iowa. Smith, of course, lived there, and Allen was born and raised there. Smith had asked Allan to deliver a letter to a mutual acquaintance who lived in Iowa. Allan, who had numerous newspaper contacts, agreed to Smith's request but also provided the letter to *The Omaha Daily Bee*. It was printed it in its entirety. The letter, published the day before the hanging, provides insight into the reasoning of Smith.[194]

Osceola, Pope County, Nebraska, July 21, 1885.

Mr. George Talbot. Old friend: Hearing where you were yesterday, I drop these few lines to you and may they find you well, but it leaves me the most miserable of the unfortunate men.

George, I came to Nebraska in 1873 and took up a homestead, and in five years I had a good farm, but about that time things turned against me and I lost all I had and am brought to the grave all though a false and treacherous and desperate woman.

She commenced her treachery 20 years ago. It was the third time she had tried it on, and it made me crazy, insane man of me.

George, if it had not been for my little children I would not be in this fix. You will find out my trouble George, and I know you can sympathize with me in my misfortune.

Your is in distress,
Milton W Smith.[195]

Between his trial and execution date, Smith was able to get two petitions signed asking the Governor to commute his sentence to life. One of the petitions was signed by four citizens and the other by eighteen. A third petition was circulated around Osceola asking the Governor not to interfere with the court's sentence.[196]

In the meantime, Sheriff Lemuel D. Hamilton prepared for the hanging by building the gallows next to the jail and erecting the proscribed enclosure to keep the scene from public view. He also went to the trouble of stringing barbed wire on the outside of the fence to keep the crowd from damaging the barricade. As the day grew near, he also became concerned about the impending crowd, and was worried that they may knock down his stockade. With this in mind, he sent a message to Governor Dawes asking for support.[197]

On July 23, 1885, Governor Dawes answered Smith's petitions and Sheriff Hamilton's request. He denied Smith's commutation and refused to send the militia.[198]

Smith had continued his bizarre behavior as late as the day before the hanging. He refused all requests to have a spiritual advisor, and continued swearing at the people of Osceola at every opportunity. He refused to have his hair cut, saying that he did not want to leave any part even a "hair in town."[199] Finally, on the night of July 23, Smith broke down and asked for a clergyman. Deacon B. C. Campbell, a prominent Methodist layman, agreed to see Smith and visited him and stayed with him until the hanging.[200]

Early in the morning of July 24, 1885, Smith had a visit from his eldest daughter, but neither of them could say a word to each other. They both cried through the entire visit. After she left, Deacon Campbell and Smith spent the rest of the morning praying.[201]

The normally resourceful Sheriff Hamilton had his hands full. The crowd gathered to view the hanging was estimated to be near 4,000, and Hamilton knew that was far too many people to manage with just his deputies. He could only hope the crowd would be orderly and not decide to tear down the scaffold. The rumor around Osceola was that after Smith was gone, the mob would take care of Smith's cellmate and neighbor, Henry Gebhardt. He was a man accused of attempting to kill his wife, but it was rumored he lacked the nerve to get the job done, unlike Smith.[202] Hamilton figured the solution to this problem was simple. He took Gebhardt from jail and rode out into the Prairie about 6 miles from town. Next, he drove a large post into the ground and chained him to the post, figuring to bring him back after the hanging.[203]

About 10:00, the crowd began pushing through the barbed wire and against the fence. Just as Hamilton had suspected, the fence was down in a matter of minutes. The crowd, however, to the Sheriff's amazement, backed off and became orderly once their vision was no longer obstructed.[204]

At 10:30, Sheriff Hamilton unlocked the cell and told Smith that his time had come. At that time, Smith's arms were bound behind him, and in the company of the Sheriff and Deacon Campbell, Smith walked to the gallows. Smith walked up the steps "showing no fear at all." The *Daily Nebraska State Journal* said, "He left all of his 58 years old there was the very object of pity when he stood on the scaffold, with his long hair and white whisker flowing in the breeze and looking out upon the crowd which covered the hillside and housetops fronting the jail."[205]

Smith was positioned on the trap door and asked if he had anything to say. He said that he was not guilty of the crime of premeditated murder. At that point, his legs were bound, the black hood was placed over his head, and the noose fashioned around his neck. He said, "I commit my spirit to God and my body to wicked people." As soon as Smith finished uttering those words, Sheriff Hamilton sprung the trap. Smith dropped 6 feet and the rope went taught and broke his neck. Blood visibly spurted from his nose. According to newspaper reports, the trap opened at 10:40 A.M. After four minutes, Dr. Hayden pronounced Smith dead, and his body was cut down and placed in the coffin just eight minutes after the execution.[206]

Osceola's saloons were closed on the morning of the execution, but opened back up when it was over. Several people filled the bars and celebrated the demise of Milton W. Smith.[207] Smith's body was buried at the expense of Polk County, and is still buried in the Osceola Cemetery.[208] Unfortunately, history is silent on where Ruth McMurphy Smith is resting.

State of Nebraska }
Polk County } ss"

Received this warrant
July 21st 1885. and I L D Hamilton,
Sheriff of said County and State, hereby
Certify that I on the 24th day of July
1885, at the hour 10 O clock and 30 minutes
A. M. after reading this Warrant to M. W.
Smith. did Execute the said Milton W
Smith. in the maner and form as in this
warrantee Commanded to do,"

This the 25th day of July 1885.

L. D. Hamilton
Sheriff of Polk Co Nebr.

Death Warrant Return - Milton W. Smith - Signed by Sheriff L. D. Hamilton

41

Smith Hanging at Osceola 1885 - Courtesy Osceola Library

Chapter IV
Jim Reynolds
The Silent Type

Chimney Rock is one of the most recognized landmarks in Nebraska. It was critical to the early pioneers using both the Oregon and Mormon Trails as they navigated their way west to the land of opportunity. Fifty miles south of Chimney Rock is the town of Sidney. It's situated about 15 miles north of the Colorado border and 50 miles east of Wyoming in the Nebraska panhandle. In 1867, it was just one more water stop poised to support the new Union Pacific Railroad.[209] Around the same time, a barracks was established at Sidney by the United States Army to protect the construction of the railroad from Indian attacks. By 1870, Fort Sidney was a complete military post and muster point, and soldiers engaging the Plains Indian tribes were quartered and regularly dispatched from the Fort. News accounts detailing the Indian campaign were routinely sent from Sidney.[210]

After the railway was firmly established and Indian hostilities somewhat curtailed, cattlemen from Texas began moving into the area, taking advantage of the wide open spaces and green grass. Sidney quickly developed into a wide open frontier town.[211] When gold was discovered in the Black Hills, Sidney became the end point of the shipping route to the gold fields near Deadwood in South Dakota. Rowdy muleskinners and teamsters were constantly coming and going through the town, the most notable of them was Calamity Jane.[212] Sidney quickly gained the reputation of being one of the wildest towns in the west. According to Loren Avey, in his book The Pole Creek Crossing, Sidney was so bad it was even referred to by the crooks, "as no more than a cesspool for every worst of the worst."[213] In 1876, things deteriorated to the point that the Union Pacific ordered trains stopping in Sidney to refuse to let people off even to stretch their legs because people were being robbed right on the platform.[214] One example of Sidney's problems happened in 1877, when a group of teamsters (wagon drivers) and a few soldiers from Fort Sidney got into a row that ended in the shooting death of a soldier named James Keith. Upon receiving the news of Keith's death, about 20 of his comrades went into Sidney and surrounded the building where the shooting took place. In concert, they began shooting volley after volley, destroying the building.[215] Sidney met the definition of an old west frontier town in all aspects. They had their share of gunfights, lynchings, cowboys, ranchers, soldiers, Indians, famous desperados, railroad robberies, and frustrated peace keepers.[216]

By 1885, Cheyenne County Sheriff Sam Fowler had helped Sidney make an about-face. The town was gradually moving from a chaotic "hell hole" to a much more stable and orderly place to live and do business. For a lot of outsiders, Cheyenne County looked as though it was a perfect place to establish a homestead.[217] Such was the case of three men who struck out for the Nebraska panhandle from Saline County in Missouri. James Pinkston was 55 years old and his son, John, was just 21. The third member of the party was 23 year old James (Jim) Reynolds, a neighbor of the Pinkston family.[218] Reynolds left his family in Missouri, and James Pinkston left his wife and 4 other children.[219]

Around the end of August, in 1885, the three men filed joint claims on land 30 miles northwest of Sidney on Middle Creek, about 20 miles southeast of Chimney Rock.[220] They made a camp, pitched a tent, and went right to the business of building a permanent dwelling. They spent nearly three weeks excavating a "dugout" and cutting lumber to be used for the front of the structure. On Wednesday, the 16th of September 1885, the three men worked hard all day. That evening, around sundown, the men were eating supper as usual in a tent, which was their temporary home.[221] For some unknown reason, they began quarreling.

Jim Reynolds ended the argument by abruptly standing up and walking out of the tent. He grabbed an axe they were using to cut logs for the exposed part of the dugout, and walked back into the tent. With a cold and calculated motion, he struck the senior Pinkston on top of the head, and then delivered a second blow to the back of his head. Next, Reynolds turned the axe on John Pinkston, and delivered a fatal blow to the back of his head. It's doubted if the elder Pinkston knew who, let alone, what hit him. John, on the other hand, was more than likely so horrified at what happened, he tried running, and that's when Reynolds struck him with the axe. Both men undoubtedly died instantly based upon the description of the bodies provided by the coroner.[222]

Reynolds quickly went to work in an attempt to cover up his crime. He hitched Pinkston's team and loaded the father and his son into their wagon. Reynolds drove the bodies approximately 1/2 mile from the camp where he found a sand pit. He unloaded the bodies and covered them with sand. Having completed this gruesome task, he returned to the camp and began digging up the ground where it was stained with the Pinkstons' blood. It's not known for sure when, but at some point between the time of the murder and when he returned to camp, Reynolds took Jim Pinkston's money. His next chore was to set fire to the tent and its contents.[223]

During the time he was hiding the bodies and burning evidence, Reynolds concocted a cover story explaining why his fellow adventurers were missing and what happened at Middle Creek camp. When he was composed and ready with his story, he unhooked the horses and set one free. Next, he mounted the remaining horse, and headed out to find someone who would listen to his tale. He rode to the nearest ranch, which coincidentally was owned by a fellow Missourian, and told the owner, Lee Nunn, what had happened.

Reynolds said that the three men had just finished supper when they were accosted in their tent by two strangers. Interestingly, he could only describe them as having black faces and pretending to be "Negros," but said he wasn't fooled by the disguise. One of the men held a cocked pistol on him, while the other struck both the elder Pinkston and his son with an axe, killing them instantly. He said they were killed because they were not forthcoming when asked about having money. He said his life was spared the same terrible fate because he immediately showed the robbers he had no money by turning his pockets inside-out. He told Nunn the murderers forced him to hitch up the team and help load the two bodies into the wagon. He continued by saying he was forced to help the men hide the bodies in a sand pit, and then ride back with them to the campsite. Nunn, who was spellbound, listened intently as Reynolds told how the robbers went back to camp and set fire to the tent. Reynolds related that when he finished the dirty work, including unhitching and chasing off the horses, the two men took the proceeds of the robbery, including Jim Pinkston's $51.00, and set off on foot in a westerly direction. Before doing so, however, they purportedly told Reynolds to "skip out," which he did. He told Nunn that he was fortunate enough to be able to capture one of the horses and ride it to his ranch.[224] Nunn put up Reynolds for the rest of the night, and in the morning, they went to Nunn's father's ranch, which was less than a mile away, and ate breakfast. After they ate and Nunn's father listened to the Reynolds story again, Lee Nunn and Jim Reynolds, at the urging of Nunn's father, headed to Sidney to report the crime to the sheriff.[225]

The entire town of Sidney was buzzing as soon as the news of the double murder hit the street. Lee Nunn told both sheriff's deputy E. T. Trognitz and Mr. Moore, the coroner, that he was not completely sold and wasn't sure that Reynolds's story was true. Moore questioned both Nunn and Reynolds in depth and asked if they had any money. Reynolds said that he had none. Moore decided to have both men detained until the stories could be checked out, and upon searching young Jim Reynolds, he found $40.00 in cash. When asked about the contradiction, Reynolds said that he found the "greenbacks" on the ground about 6 miles outside of town. He also told Moore he lied about not having any money after Nunn told him that if he told his story about finding the money, he would be a suspect in the murders. The deputy then asked Reynolds to take off his boots. Trognitz found a bloody pocketbook containing $15.00 in one of them.[226] Both Trognitz and Moore believed that Reynolds's story about the two mystery robbers was absurd. Coupled with the fact that he had so much cash in his possession, they were sure that Reynolds was the actual murderer.[227]

Lee Nunn was asked if he was familiar with the area. He was asked, based on Reynolds's story, if he could show Coroner Moore and Deputy Trognitz where the camp was possibly located. He was also asked to direct them to the sandpits described by Reynolds where the bodies could be buried. Several citizens from Sidney accompanied the men first to the crime scene and eventually to the sandpits where they found the burial site. The bodies of John and Jim Pinkston were recovered and examined. A physical examination of the dead men cast an even greater shadow on Reynolds's story as far as the coroner was concerned, and his next step was to conduct a coroner's inquest. He gathered a jury from the onlookers who were still at the crime scene, and right there and then, on the prairie, conducted an inquiry. The jury quickly came back and said the Pinkstons were murdered and pointed the finger at Jim Reynolds, alleging the crime was first degree murder.[228] On September 17, 1885, Justice of the Peace Robert Shuman issued an arrest warrant and deputy Trognitz took Reynolds into custody.[229]

Sheriff Fowler, who had returned to Cheyenne County, was keenly aware that the citizens of Sidney were not bashful about lynching someone and feared that Reynolds might be a candidate for a necktie party if left in the county jail. So, when Jim Reynolds was arrested, he was taken to the village of Lodgepole, about 18 miles east of Sidney, for safekeeping.[230]

Reynolds was eventually returned to Sidney to await legal proceedings. As soon as he was jailed, he began limiting his conversations and ultimately stopped talking altogether. He quickly became very sullen. His behavior created the impression that he may be insane.[231] He was scheduled to go on trial on December 28, 1885, in the Cheyenne District Court before Judge Francis G. Hamer, but the issue of his sanity was raised. Reynolds was described as having "nervous spells."[232] Judge Hamer ordered him examined by a panel of doctors and then held a sanity hearing to determine if he was fit for trial. All 5 physicians, who each conducted an examination, testified that he was sane, and the judge ordered the trial to proceed.[233] The trial began on schedule.

The prosecutor was H. M. Sinclair, the 10th judicial district attorney from Plum Creek, and Reynolds's court appointed defense attorneys were W. C. Reilly of Sidney and Charles Reilly of Kearney. The trial began with jury selection. Mr. Sinclair did not object to a single juror, and Reynolds's defense team only excused 5 men, resulting in an expeditious jury selection.[234]

Sinclair wasted little time after his opening remarks, and quickly built a circumstantial case. Next, he called several witnesses who each testified that Reynolds had made a confession to them sometime shortly after his arrest.[235] Reynolds did not take the stand in his defense, and his attorneys said that "if he could speak," he would testify that there was a quarrel between the men and that his actions were simply a man defending himself.[236]

Judge Hamer read instructions to the jury panel at 10:00 P.M. on December 31, 1885, New Year's Eve. Before the New Year, just two hours later, the jury had returned a verdict of murder in the first degree on both charges. Judge Hamer pronounced sentence and set the date of May 21, 1886 as the date for James Reynolds's hanging. All this was accomplished before midnight.[237]

Reynolds spent the next three months in the Cheyenne County jail, exhibiting the same silent behavior he did before his trial. Meanwhile, on January 5, 1885, Cheyenne County had a new Sheriff, William T. Eubanks. He had the job of overseeing Reynolds's hanging. Besides the logistical tasks, such as constructing the gallows and stockade, a major concern of the sheriff was that Reynolds may be insane and, according to the court order, it was his duty to hang him. On Monday, May 17, 1886, Sheriff Eubanks took his problem to Governor Dawes. The Governor decided that he would ask Dr. Matthewson, who had examined Reynolds before the trial, to re-examine him. Governor Dawes decided that any executive action he took would be based upon the advice of Dr. Matthewson and his conclusions surrounding Reynolds's sanity.[238]

On the 18th of May, the Tuesday before the scheduled hanging, Dr. Matthewson did examine Reynolds. It was determined that if he found that Reynolds was insane, it should be the duty of the courts, specifically Judge Hamer in this case, to set aside Reynolds's hanging, not Governor Dawes. Clemency could be considered by the Governor, but it would be separate from the issue of Reynolds's sanity.[239] Therefore, Judge Hamer decided to seat a jury to hear the outcome of his medical (psychiatric) examination. Drs. Matthewson and O. J. Carter spent the entire day with Reynolds. They gave him both chloroform and ether, and after he was sufficiently under the influence of the drugs, he broke his silence and talked to the doctors about his crime and other topics. They let Reynolds talk for over an hour. At the conclusion of the exam, both doctors testified before the jury that Jim Reynolds was sane. The jury deliberated only short time, and declared that Reynolds was sane and could be executed on Friday.[240]

Reynolds didn't sleep the night before the execution, and spent his last night talking with his spiritual advisor, Reverend E. Stevens. In the morning, reverend Stevens performed a baptism for Reynolds. Reynolds in turn gave Stevens a statement saying that all of the news accounts of the incident were correct in almost every detail, which amounted to a public, last minute confession. Richards requested that ex-sheriff Fowler, along with Sheriff Eubanks, attend the hanging.[241] Richards then decided to write a letter to his family.

Dear folks at home: Before this reaches you I will be in eternity. I am executed today for the taking the life of James Pinkston and his son. I did it not intentionally. There was a foolish dispute about a settlement which resulted in the killing. The minister sends you a paper with my statement, which is correct in every particular. I have kept nothing back. The sentence is too severe but is lawful.

With the help of God I will die like a Man. I have made my peace. Don't grieve, for life is short and full of sorrow and sin. Watch your tempers that they don't lead you through the path of mine. I give George Keep my Colt in memory of my unfortunate brother. I send in my ring to Dollie. Keep it for life as a dying brother's wish. Don't grieve for me.

Signed - James Reynolds.[242]

Sheriff Eubanks came for Jim Reynolds shortly after 3 P.M., and seemed nervous as he read the death warrant in a shaky voice. Reynolds, on the other hand, was calm, and said that he "intended to die game."[243] Reynolds was dressed in a black suit and reporters described him as being nearly 6 feet tall and weighing less than 150 pounds.[244]

Around 3:20 P.M., Reynolds was taken from his cell by Sheriff Eubanks and Deputy Sheriff Moore and escorted to the scaffold. They were accompanied by ex-sheriff Fowler and Reverend Stevens. At 3:22 P.M., the procession, consisting of Reynolds, Sheriff Eubanks, Deputy Moore, the Reverend Stevens, and Samuel Fowler, started for the scaffold. It was located on the west side of the jail and described as being 7 feet high and approximately 12 foot square with the trap door situated directly in the center.[245]

Reynolds walked up the steps showing no outward signs of emotion and without hesitation stepped on the trap door. Sheriff Eubanks quickly tied his arms and legs and placed the noose around his neck. He was asked if he had any last words. He looked at Reverend Stevens and said, "make a good prayer for me, and then when you get through I want to go."[246] Before the prayer was finished, the trap door was sprung and Jim Reynolds, as the headline read in *The Omaha Herald*, "expiated his crime."[247] In 13 minutes, the doctors in attendance, including Dr. Matthewson, declared Reynolds dead, and the body was cut down and placed in a wooden coffin. Jim Reynolds's body was put on display in front of the jail, and after the spectators had a good look, he was buried in Boot Hill, all before 5 P.M. that evening.[248]

An interesting rumor circulated around Sidney shortly after the hanging. The story was that Sheriff Eubanks did not want to pull the lever controlling the trap door so he paid a 15 year old boy $5.00 to do the job. It was 35 years before the rumor was finally dispelled. A letter written in 1922, from O. D. Lyon, was sent from California to the *Sidney Telegraph* newspaper. Lyon was a former Sidney citizen and witness to the execution. The letter verified that Sheriff Eubanks did not pull the lever, but also noted it was not a 15 year old boy that did the job. Lyon's assertion was that a man named Miller, who happened to be in Sidney at the time selling horses, was paid $5.00 by Eubanks to pull the lever. Lyon's letter was prompted by a news story retelling the account of the hanging. The event was back in the news because several bodies from Sidney's Boot Hill cemetery were being moved.[249]

The cemetery was used by the Army for soldiers stationed at Fort Sidney, and most were buried during the time of the Indian wars. In 1922, 200 bodies, mostly soldiers, were moved from Boot Hill to Fort McPherson national cemetery.[250] Some civilians buried at Boot Hill were also moved to Fort McPherson, including James and John Pinkston. Jim Reynolds, however, remains buried in Boot Hill.[251]

Chimney Rock Near Bayard, NE - (ca 1906)

Front St. - Sidney, Nebraska (ca 1900) Courtesy Cheyenne County Historical Society

JAMES PINKSTON   JOHN PINKSTON

James Reynolds

Judge Hamer

Warrant.

The State of Nebraska ⎫
Cheyenne County ⎬ ss

The State of Nebraska to all Sheriffs, Constables and Coroners of said State Greeting: It appearing that James Reynolds has committed the crime of felonious murder on the persons of James Pinkston and John Pinkston in the County of Cheyenne, you are therefor commanded to forthwith arrest James Reynolds and bring him before me or some other Magistrate of Cheyenne County, to be dealt with according to law.

Given under my hand this 17th day of September A. D. 1885.

Robert Shuman, Justice of the Peace

Return of Warrant.

Reynolds arrest record

Sidney, Cheyenne County - 1868
The Denver Public Library, Western History Collection-Call Z-5818

Chapter V
William Jackson Marion
Injustice

In 1880, the Commissioner of Indian Affairs issued his annual report to the Secretary of the Interior. The report describes the Otoe Indian reservation as, "43,000 fertile acres, said to be better watered, wooded, and generally adapted to agriculture than any other part of the State. The land is gently rolling, easily cultivated, and produces luxuriant crops of hay and corn, wheat not flourishing in the same proportion. It is located in southern Gage County, Nebraska, is about 6 miles in width and 10 miles in length, extending a distance of 2 miles into the State of Kansas."[252]

The reservation was a perfect place for the home of the Otoe Indians, but many others, mostly railroads, thought it was a perfect place for them too. In 1870, the tribe survived an attempt by the St. Louis and Nebraska Railroad Trunk to buy the land.[253] The federal government finally prevailed, and by 1882, the Nebraska Otoe reservation, or Otoe Agency as it was called, was no more. The Otoe tribe was relocated to Indian Territory in Oklahoma.[254] During the 1870s, however, while the Otoe tribe was still on their reservation, it was the scene of one of Nebraska's most curious murder mysteries.

Both the Union Pacific Railroad and Burlington and Missouri Railroad built lines near the agency.[255] Another line, the St. Joseph & Denver City Railroad, extended northwest through Kansas and up into Nebraska, eventually making connections possible with the other two lines. The St. Joseph & Denver City line ran parallel to the Little Blue River through Steel City, Nebraska, near a point which literally abutted the western edge of the Otoe reservation.[256] On the eastern border of the reservation, approximately 30 miles east of Steel City, was the town of Liberty, Nebraska.

John and Rachel Warren lived near Wolf Creek, near the small town of Liberty, which was in southern Gage County, Nebraska. The couple's daughter, Lydia Jane Finley, was married to William

Jackson Marion, known as "Jack" to his friends. She was Rachel's natural daughter from her previous marriage. In 1871, the Marion couple lived in Kansas in the town of Grasshopper Falls, situated in Jefferson County about 100 miles southeast of where the Warrens lived. In 1872, the beginning of the story, Jack and Lydia Marion had been married less than a year. He was a 23 year old unemployed railroad worker, who was said to be illiterate. It was rumored, to put it nicely, that he was somewhat of a scoundrel. His wife was once told that her husband killed a man in Indian Territory, and escaped from the Cherokee Nation's jail.[257] That fact was never verified, but it added to Jack's bad reputation.

The couple had a 20 year old friend, John Cameron, who boarded with them for a short time in Grasshopper Falls. In the Spring of 1872, John Cameron and Jack Marion decided to go to Steel City in Nebraska and work on the St. Joseph & Denver City Railroad. Before leaving Kansas, however, Cameron agreed to sell his team of horses and harness to Marion for $225.00, and gave him $30.00 as a down payment. The day before the two men left, Marion also bought Cameron's wagon and agreed to pay $90.00 for it when they found work.[258]

Sometime in April 1872, Jack and Lydia Marion, along with Cameron, made their way to the Warren home near Liberty. The two men took advantage of the Warrens' hospitality while they planned their trip west. On May 3, 1872, Cameron and Jack Marion struck out for Steel City with the intent of finding work, leaving Lydia with her parents. Lydia expected the men to be gone at least several weeks, but on May 6, Jack Marion returned alone, driving the team he purchased from Cameron. When asked about Cameron, Marion said that the two decided to go their separate ways, and Cameron bid him goodbye and went to Clay County, Kansas where he had relatives. According to his mother-in-law, Rachel Warren, Jack also brought back most of Cameron's belongings, including the clothing she had washed and packed for Cameron shortly before the trip. Rachel also noticed that Jack was wearing Cameron's new boots.[259] There was a good deal of speculation that Marion's story was less than truthful and that Cameron was dead and Jack ended up with a stolen team, wagon, and Cameron's belongings. According to Lydia, Marion's father, Tipton Marion, who also lived near Liberty, told Jack to go back and find work on the railroad if he was innocent of any foul play involving Cameron, but if he was guilty, his advice was to "just keep going."[260]

On March 14, 1873, just over 10 months after Jack returned to Liberty without Cameron, a German immigrant named Kleinhunts found human remains on Indian Creek near Steel City. The Gage county coroner, Job Buchanan, went to the scene with several others and found a human skull and skeleton of an adult man. The coroner speculated that the remains were more than likely those of the missing John Cameron. He quickly determined, however, that the remains were actually just over the county line in Jefferson County, and subsequently notified the Jefferson County authorities. Less than a week later, however, on March 19, a man named Harris was traveling the road running from Steel City to Beatrice, and approximately 6 miles from where Kleinhunts made his discovery, Harris found another human skull and a partially buried body. The location of the second body was definitely in Gage County and happened to be on the Otoe Reservation. The skull found by Harris had three unmistakable bullet holes in it. Job Buchanan again went out, this time with Harris, and located the rest of the remains.[261] The coroner brought the skeleton and the remnants of the clothing back to Beatrice.[262]

On Saturday the 22nd of March, 1873, Job Buchanan impaneled a coroner's jury to investigate the circumstances surrounding the second body. John Warren, Jack's father-in-law, was first to testify. He testified that the remains looked like John Cameron, the man who left his residence with Jackson Marion and never returned. He described Cameron, what he was wearing the last time he saw him, and noted that his hair color was light brown, the same as the residual hair on the skeleton.[263]

Jack's wife, Lydia, testified next. She said she asked her husband why he was wearing Cameron's boots and some of his clothing. He simply replied that Cameron's boots were newer and his were nearly worn out with no other explanation. Lydia testified that Marion brought back Cameron's writing instruments and paper as well, and said she told Jack that she thought he killed Cameron. The last thing Lydia told the jury was that she hadn't seen or heard from her husband since their conversation in May of 1872.[264]

It didn't take long for the jury to decide that the body discovered by Harris was John Cameron, based upon John Warren's identification and the familiar clothing and hair color. It also determined that Cameron met his death after suffering three gunshot wounds to the head. The jury considered the circumstance of Marion's return to Liberty with Cameron's team and the jury's verdict was that Jack Marion was the perpetrator.

Buchanan's statement was, "there is little room to doubt the correctness of this verdict, either as to the identity of the murdered man or the fixing of the crime upon Marion."[265] A warrant was issued for William Jackson Marion's arrest.[266] Jack, however, apparently listened to his father's advice and just kept going.

In December of 1882, 10½ years after Cameron and Marion left for Steel City, a man from Beatrice, the capital of Gage County, was in jail in Sedan, Kansas. Sedan is the capital of Chautauqua County, which is a south-central county sharing its southern border with the State of Oklahoma.[267] In 1882, however, Chautauqua County was also just a step away from Indian Territory, notoriously known at the time as a refuge for wanted criminals.[268] Jack Marion was also in jail at Sedan in December of 1882. He was awaiting trial on a theft charge, accused of stealing a wagon. Unfortunately for William Jackson Marion, the man from Beatrice was acquainted with him and knew he was wanted. As soon as he recognized Jack, without hesitation, Marion's fellow prisoner wrote a letter to Gage County Sheriff, Captain Nathanial Herron.[269]

Nathaniel Herron, a Civil War veteran elected sheriff in 1880, wasted no time in heading for Sedan. Kansas authorities agreed to let Marion plead guilty to the theft charge, stipulating that Herron would extradite him back to Nebraska. On Saturday evening, December 30, 1882, Sheriff Herron was back in Beatrice and Marion was in the Gage County jail. On Tuesday January 9, Marion appeared before Judge Kretsing and pled not guilty to the charge.[270] On April 20, 1883, Marion was indicted by a Gage County grand jury for the murder of John Cameron, which occurred nearly 11 years earlier.[271]

William Jackson Marion's murder trial began on May 3, 1883 in Gage County District Court before Judge S. P. Davidson. The prosecution was handled by district attorney R. W. Sabin and attorney Robert S. Bibb. The defense counsel for Marion was Leonard W. Colby.[272]

After the prosecution established that the body, which had been found ten years earlier, was John Cameron, they also needed to prove the death was a result of the bullet wounds to the head. Now it was time for Sabin and Bibb to begin stacking up their circumstantial case. Jacob Worley, Marion's landlord in Grasshopper Falls, testified that in 1872, he was present when the agreement was made between Marion and Cameron over the purchase of the team and wagon.[273]

Rachel Warren, Jack's mother-in-law, testified that the two men stayed with her a few days while they made preparations to go west. She testified that she washed Cameron's clothes and her husband put the clothing in a trunk. She said she also saw a new pair of fancy boots belonging to Cameron, and she overheard Jack make an offer to buy the boots from Cameron, which he refused. She also testified that Marion had a revolver, which he repaired and test fired before the two men departed. Rachel testified that she watched as the pair left for Steel City, and also noted in her testimony that Cameron was wearing his new boots.[274]

John Warren, Rachel's husband, also testified that he was at home three days later when Jack came back by himself. He testified Marion was driving the team of mares belonging to Cameron. He said Jack was wearing Cameron's fancy boots; the same ones Cameron was wearing when he left. Warren asked Marion what had happened to his partner, to which he replied he last saw him at Blue Springs when the men parted company. Warren testified that he got up early the next morning and checked the Marion's wagon noticing that he also returned with Cameron's trunk. Looking inside, he noticed that the clothing was still intact and just as it was when he packed it. He testified that on the 19th of May, 1872, Marion left his residence headed towards Pawnee County, and said, "I never saw him until I saw him now." Lastly, he told the jury he once overheard Jack talking to Lydia about Cameron. He said Marion told her he could probably find Cameron, but it would cost "a damn sight to find him."[275]

The defense couldn't mount a viable defense, so Marion testified and essentially repeated the story of the two men parting company. He said that when the men reached the Little Blue River, they found the wages were too low, and Cameron decided to go to Kansas and see his uncle. Marion said he decided to return to the area of Pawnee County and look for work. Marion said that Cameron asked him to take his trunk back and said the men planned on meeting later when they found work. He said the last time he saw Cameron, he was headed south into Kansas with some other travelers headed in the same direction.[276]

Although the prosecution's case was based solely on circumstantial evidence, the jury wasted little time in returning a verdict of guilty of murder in the first degree against Marion. He was sentenced by Judge Davidson to be hung on September 7, 1883.[277]

Jack Marion's attorney asked for reconsideration of the verdict and moved for a new trial, but was swiftly denied. He subsequently appealed to the Nebraska Supreme Court, citing several errors but strongly asserting that Nebraska's courts actually lacked jurisdiction to hear the case. He based the argument upon the fact that the body purported to be that of John Cameron was actually found on the Otoe Indian reservation and, if anything, it was a federal case. The court rejected the argument that the court lacked jurisdiction but instead ruled in Marion's favor on one of the minor issues. On cross examination, the prosecution asked Marion if he pled guilty to a felony in Kansas shortly before his extradition to Nebraska. Although his attorney objected, Marion was forced to answer yes. The Supreme Court ruled that based upon the facts, the question was improper and Judge Davidson should have sustained the objection. On August 8, 1884, the court reversed Judge Davidson's denial for a new trial and remanded the case for further proceedings.[278]

The second trial of William Jackson Marion began on March 3, 1885 before Judge Jefferson H. Broady. The prosecution team consisted of District Attorney D. J. Osgood and Robert S. Bibb. Marion was defended by Leonard W. Colby and Charles O. Bates. The State's case was presented essentially the same as the first, with the most damaging testimony, once again, coming from Marion's in-laws. The trial lasted all day and was reconvened after the supper hour at 7:30 PM. Closing arguments and jury instructions were completed, and the jury retired at 9:00 PM. The jury deliberation took only 45 minutes and returned a verdict of guilty in the first degree with a recommendation that the judge sentence Marion to hang.[279]

On Saturday, March 7, 1885, William Jackson Marion appeared before Judge Broady for sentencing. The judge conducted a lengthy sermon before pronouncing the sentence. He began by saying, "They that sow to the wind will reap the whirlwind." When he finished, he said Marion was to be confined until the 26th day of June; then taken by the sheriff to the place of execution and between the hours of 9 and 1 O'clock be hanged by the neck until, "dead dead dead!"[280]

Marion's attorneys, Colby and Bates, added attorney Alfred Hazlett to the defense team. They once again asked for and were denied a new trial, and once again they appealed the District Judge's decision to the Nebraska Supreme Court. Nebraska's high court issued a stay of execution on June 15, 1885.[281] The court entertained a litany of arguments from Marion's defense team.

The majority attacked testimonial evidence that established the strong circumstantial case. They also challenged the introduction of a photograph of Cameron purportedly used for identification purposes. The attorneys gathered several affidavits from witnesses swearing they saw one of the members of the jury drinking whiskey in a saloon before court and then used the fact that the juror was intoxicated during the trial as an appeal issue.[282]

On October 27, 1886, the Supreme Court issued its ruling. "Finding no error in the record to prejudice of plaintiff in error, the judgment of the district court must be affirmed, which is done." The court's summary sealed the fate of William Jackson Marion, accused, tried, and now convicted of murdering his friend nearly 14½ years earlier. The Supreme Court also set a new execution date. Marion was scheduled to be hung on March 11, 1887.[283]

Marion was once again placed in the Gage County jail. It had been his home for nearly 4 years. The jail was described as being 30 feet by 31 feet and containing 6 cells. The jail was completed and opened in the early part of 1874.[284] In terms of security, the jail was certainly not escape proof. On June 6, 1874, two men broke out of the new jail and made off with two horses from a nearby farm to make their escape.[285] A week later on June 13, 1874, Taylor Tucedell, who was also a horse thief, escaped from the new jail.[286] Many of the citizens of Beatrice wondered why Jack Marion, a man who had a track record of taking it on the lam, did not at least make an attempt to break jail, unless, of course, he was innocent.[287]

Sometime in February, 1887, a petition was circulated in Gage County asking the Governor to commute Marion's sentence from death to life imprisonment. Nearly 1,000 persons signed the petition. The population of Gage County according to the 1890 United States Census was 30,000 persons.[288] After careful consideration, on March 8, 1887, Governor Thayer sent word that he would not commute the sentence and rescheduled the execution for March 25, 1887.[289] The Governor, however, left the door open by not addressing the clemency petition.

As the date of Jack Marion's execution grew close, Governor John Thayer sent Sheriff E. F. Davis a note indicating that, although he had yet to make a decision regarding clemency, the Sheriff should take all necessary steps to proceed with the hanging. The sheriff complied and on Tuesday, March 22, 1887, he began building the scaffold and privacy fence behind the jail. In addition, he had admission passes printed which read, "Admit holder of this ticket to the execution of Jackson Marion, Friday,

March 25, 1887, as assistant," and was signed, "E. F. Davis, Sheriff."[290] The work was completed and the area, which was described as 40' by 60' surrounded by a tight 16' high fence, abutted the jail on the east side. The scaffold was described as having a 12' by 16' floor and being 8' high. The trap door was 4' by 4' in the center of the scaffold. Jack Marion was just a few feet away from the construction listening to the sounds of the hammers as they built his gallows.[291]

On Wednesday evening, March 23, 1887, Captain J. E. Hill, a Governor Thayer aide, personally carried a letter to Sheriff Davis. The letter indicated that Thayer had made a decision, and that, "he declined to interfere with the sentence," and ordered the sheriff to proceed with the execution as scheduled for the following Friday. The Governor did authorize 500 National Guard troops to assist the sheriff in maintaining order.[292]

On Thursday evening, Attorney Hazlett along with a stenographer paid a visit to the jail, and asked if Marion would like to make a statement. Jack's statement was clear and concise. He said, "I don't know as if I have anything to say, except only that, I did not kill that man." After Hazlett left, Marion ate a "hearty" supper and spent several hours with Reverend G. H. Albright, pastor of Trinity Lutheran Church and Jack's spiritual advisor.[293]

At 11:00 A.M., Friday the 25th of March, 1887, after a brief religious service, Sheriff Davis read the death warrant to Marion. Jack was calm and unaffected.[294] At 11:05, Sheriff Davis, Reverend Albright, Marion, and several others walked into the enclosure and up the steps of the scaffold. About 150 people were crowded into the area to watch the hanging. Sheriff Davis asked Marion if he had any last words as Jack stood there with the noose dangling in front of him. He said no at first, and then both Davis and Albright stepped up and spoke to him in a soft tone only heard by Marion. He then said in a strong voice, "We'll gentleman," and continued by emphasizing that the reason he had not made a confession was that he was not guilty and did not kill Cameron. He acknowledged being a "sinner," but said he was just like most others. He finished by saying, "God help everybody; that's including everybody."[295] The only relative in attendance was Jack's uncle, William Wymore, who lived in the area. He was allowed to ascend the steps of the gallows and say goodbye. He talked momentarily with Jack and shook his hand. At 11:18, the sheriff placed the noose around Jack's neck and then put the black hood over his head. At 11:20, the sheriff gave a signal and the trap door was sprung by someone inside the jail. A steel rod running through the wall of the jail served as a lever for the trap door and kept the executioner out of sight.[296] Marion's neck was broken immediately and he died without a tremor.[297] Jack Marion was declared dead after hanging about 15 minutes, and at 11:45 A.M., the body was cut down and placed outside of the enclosure for the public to view. It was estimated that 1,000 people walked past and viewed the body. Just 15 minutes later, William Jackson Marion was placed in a coffin and taken away. Marion was buried at 4:00 P.M. in potter's field.[298]

The story of William Jackson Marion does not end in potter's field. William Wymore, Jack's uncle, unquestionably believed that Jack was not guilty of murdering John Cameron. Oddly, Wymore not only believed that his nephew didn't kill Cameron; he also believed that Cameron was still alive. After a few years of making inquiries, Wymore picked up stories that Cameron was alive and was seen in La Crosse, Kansas. He immediately went to Kansas and searched the area, but could not locate him. Sometime later, he again heard the rumors and went back to La Crosse and subsequently located John Cameron, well and alive. Wymore and Jack's brother, Dub, sat down and talked with Cameron in La Crosse, and asked him what happened when the two men left Liberty.[299]

Cameron said that he left Marion in the company of another person near the Blue River and traveled to Mexico. He stayed there several years working in the mines, and then struck out for California. From there he headed to Alaska and worked there until he decided to go to Colorado. He said it was only then, about a year ago, that he learned of Marion's fate on the gallows. He said he was frightened of the fact that he may be held responsible for Jack's death, and tried to keep out of sight. When he was asked why he left so abruptly, he said a girl was going to "swear a child on me." When he was asked about the team and the clothing he said, that he was still in possession of Marion's promissory note and that he traded some of his clothes to an Indian for some blankets.[300]

Wymore took his story to the newspapers and swore that he and Marion's brother positively identified Cameron. When he was asked why Cameron did not come back with him to Beatrice, his response was that he was still frightened that he could be legally held responsible for Marion's death, even after he received assurances from Wymore. Wymore stated that if need be, he was sure he could locate Cameron again.[301]

The best information available says that there was no second interview of Cameron, and no attempt made to bring him back to Beatrice. Not doing so left several questions unanswered. Who was with Jack Marion when the two men parted company, and who was the person found with three bullet holes in their skull? Even if Cameron traded his clothing to an Indian, it is doubtful if the Indian had light brown hair. Did the Warren's use the circumstances to extract some type of retribution from Marion?

An editorial in the Saturday edition of the *Omaha Daily Bee*, March 26, 1887, the day after the hanging simply said, "It might be safe to say that capital punishment punishes."[302] Exactly one hundred years later, after a protracted effort by the family, Governor Bob Kerrey of Nebraska issued a full pardon to W. J. Marion.[303]

W. J. Marion

William Jackson Marion
Courtesy Gage County Historical Society

Gage County Jail Razing - 1918

The Hanging of William Jackson Marion
Courtesy of the Gage County Historical Society and Museum

Chapter VI
David Hoffman
A Real Train Wreck

In the spring of 1886, the Missouri Pacific Railway system employed over 14,000 people. In March of that year, the company became embroiled in what would be later known as *The Great Strike of 1886*.[304] The company suspended 6,095 workers that month and an additional 3,000 sympathetic employees walked off the job.[305] The strike turned deadly for the railroad on April 26, 1886 at Wyandotte, Kansas, when engine 892 pulling a load of freight cars plunged into the Kansas River, killing two members of the crew. The wreck was a result of sabotage. Witnesses saw three men running from the scene, and the initial investigation determined deliberately loosened tracks caused the wreck.[306] Three men were arrested for the crime, but after several protracted trials, they were all acquitted.[307] The last of the accused, George Hamilton, was acquitted at his second trial in September of 1887, a full year after the *Great Strike* was settled.[308]

On January 11, 1887, a bitterly cold snowy evening, a similar train wreck occurred near the small village of Dunbar, Nebraska, sending a southbound Missouri Pacific passenger train plummeting off the tracks. The engineer, James Dewitt, was killed, and the express man, Frank Chenowith, was critically injured. The train carried 87 passengers, of which at least half sustained injuries, some more serious than others.[309] Since DeWitt was from Wyandotte and supported management's position during the strike, Missouri Pacific officials were quick to jump to the conclusion that the wreck was aimed at DeWitt, and it was an act of retribution committed by the Knights of Labor.[310] The Knights of Labor was one of the first major labor organizations of America's burgeoning labor movement. After all, first reports, just like in Kansas, said witnesses saw two men fleeing the scene, and the tracks removed just like those at Wyandotte. Otoe County Sheriff George R. MaCallum and Missouri Pacific detectives quickly dispelled the railroad's theory. It wasn't labor strife that was the motive for the dastardly act, just plain greed. The express car guarded by Chenowith was carrying $17,000 in bullion.[311]

The snowpack, which was also credited with cushioning the impact of the train's 15 foot drop, yielded perfect footprints of the two men who fled the scene. It was a simple task for investigators to track the perpetrators through a cornfield and to the home of John Hoffman.[312] Hoffman's brother, David, and his friend, James W. Bell, were at the house and seemed nervous. Hoffman was staying with his brother, helping him with the farm chores, and his friend Bell was a farmer from Unadilla, a small community to the west. Missouri Pacific detectives Frank Tutt and John DeLong, along with Sheriff MaCallum and County Coroner Frederick H. Brauer, noticed several inconsistencies in their stories when they were questioned. Investigators took the men's boots and matched them to the footprints leading from the wreck to the house. David Hoffman was wearing a pair of rubber boots with a distinctive patch on the sole. The boots and the prints were an exact match.[313]

County coroner F. H. Brauer wasted no time impaneling a jury to conduct an inquest into the wreck and DeWitt's death. The jury quickly determined that the engineer's death was a homicide and that Hoffman and Bell were responsible. As soon as David Hoffman and James Bell were arrested, the citizens of Dunbar began buzzing, and talked about lynching the two men. Sheriff McCallum quickly put an end to the idea of having "Judge Lynch" resolve the matter, and took the two prisoners to the Otoe County jail in Nebraska City.[314] The village of Dunbar, with a population of 208 in 1887, is 10 miles west of Nebraska City, and Unadilla is 13 miles west of Dunbar. In 1887, Unadilla, Bell's home, had approximately 300 residents. Both men were well known in both Dunbar and Unadilla. They spent a great deal of time drinking in Moffat's Saloon, a local bar. Even before their arrest, neither man was too well liked. Sheriff McCallum, however, was confident that the two were safe in the Otoe county jail.[315]

On Thursday evening, the 13th of January, the two suspects were taken from the county jail to a room in the Grand Pacific Hotel in Nebraska City by Missouri Pacific detective Frank Tutt and the sheriff. The two were questioned separately, and each made a full confession of the crime. The railroad detectives and the sheriff were elated because, for all intents and purposes, the case of the Dunbar train wreck and murder was solved.[316] District Attorney John C. Watson presented his case to the grand jury and both men were, without hesitation, indicted for the crime of first degree murder. The pair was taken before Judge Mapes and bound over for trial in the next session of the District Court scheduled for the following spring. Hoffman and Bell were represented by A. S. Cole and Charles W. Seymour; two well-known Nebraska City attorneys. District Attorney John C. Watson represented the State with the assistance of D. T. Hayden, another prominent Nebraska City attorney. The case was heard in front of the Honorable Samuel M. Chapman.[317]

Before the trial began, attorneys for both defendants made a pretrial motion alleging that the confessions, which actually cemented the case for the prosecution, were illegally obtained. Hoffman said that on the night of January 13, 1887, Sheriff McCallum and his deputy, Joseph Huberlee, took him to the Grand Pacific Hotel along with Bell. He said the two were separated and questioned individually. He was asked to describe the method used during questioning. He said an unknown man, believed to be a railroad detective, took out his pistol and cocked it, then placed it to his head. The detective then asked another man, also believed to be a railroad detective to take out his watch. Hoffman then said that the man told him he had 2 minutes to decide if he should or shouldn't confess to his involvement in the crime. If, said the man, he (Hoffman) decided to remain quiet, then he would blow a hole in Hoffman's head. Hoffman then said he decided that he would rather not have his head blown off, and confessed to the crime. Hoffman testified that Sheriff McCallum and his deputy were present during the questioning and did nothing to stop the coercion. James Bell told a similar story.[318]

Judge Chapman overruled the motion, and ruled the trial should go forward. The two men then asked for separate trials, and the judge agreed. Hoffman's trial would be first, followed by Bell's. The jury for David Hoffman's case was seated by the end of the day, and opening arguments scheduled for the following day, April 8, 1887.[319]

Testimony began with a description of the wreck by passengers and the train crew. Missouri Pacific officials that coincidentally were on the train on the night of the incident also told of terrible way in which James DeWitt died. The express manager, Frank Chenowith, told the jury of his near death injuries. He said the wreck caused a small steel safe to be hurled across the car, striking him in the head. The jury was able to see a large scar on his forehead that was not entirely healed. Investigators told the court how they followed the tracks in the snow from the wreck to John Hoffman's house, and subsequently matched the boots of David Hoffman and James Bell to the tracks. Frank Tutt, the chief investigator for the Missouri Pacific, testified that he questioned Hoffman at the Grand Pacific Hotel on the night of the 13th of January and provided, in detail, the sequence of events based upon Hoffman's confession.[320]

The most damaging testimony came the following day when the defense team's fears were recognized. James Bell decided to turn state's evidence and testify against Hoffman. His testimony, it was feared, would corroborate Frank Tutt's testimony. Bell's testimony was, for the most part, a repeat of his confession at the Grand Pacific Hotel. The exception, of course, being that his story on the witness stand mitigated his involvement and aggravated Hoffman's.[321]

Bell began by saying about 10 O'clock, he and Hoffman started for John Hoffman's house; but when they were walking near the B & M section house, where the tools were kept, Hoffman told him a passenger train carrying a good deal of money would be down the Missouri Pacific shortly. According to Bell, Hoffman said he had a switch key which would open the section house, but when he tried it, he could not get the door open. He was very specific, saying at that point Hoffman forced the door and removed "a claw bar and wrench." They then walked to the Missouri Pacific tracks. Bell said he was so drunk that he could not help and only watched as Hoffman removed the bolts and plate holding the rail in place. He said he asked Hoffman what he was doing and Hoffman replied, "I'm going to wreck the dammed train and get the money." When the last plate was removed and the rail loosened, they saw the train coming, and ran towards the woods. Bell said the two men stopped and watched as the train left the tracks and headed down the embankment into the snow. He said they could hear sounds of the derailing cars, the steam escaping from the boiler, and the screams of the passengers. He continued by saying they were too frightened to go back and make an attempt to get the money, so they ran through the woods to John Hoffman's house. Bell was adamant that his participation was only minimal.[322]

The only hope for the defense was to let David Hoffman tell his side of the story. Hoffman took the stand the following day and essentially gave a similar account of the incident. In Hoffman's version, however, it was James Bell who masterminded the plot, and he was the drunken follower. It was a case of the two men pointing the finger at each other, and the defense felt Hoffman was more believable than Bell. They sincerely expected the jury would think so too. Apparently they were wrong because jury deliberation took all of 30 minutes, and their verdict was that Hoffman was guilty of murder in the first degree. Hoffman was visibly shaken when the foreman read the verdict. His attorneys filed a motion for a new trial, which was promptly denied by Judge Chapman. David Hoffman turned 24 years old just two days before the Judge Chapman sentenced him to hang. He openly cried when he heard the sentence; knowing full well he would not live to see his 25th birthday. He was scheduled to be executed on July 22, 1887.[323]

The day after Hoffman's trial, James Bell pled guilty to a lesser charge of murder, and was sentenced by Judge Chapman to 10 years in the Nebraska Penitentiary. Both the prosecution and the Missouri Pacific detectives painted a picture of Bell as being a drunken dupe who was used by Hoffman. They unofficially suggested a 7 year sentence would be fair, but the Judge disagreed mainly because talk within the community was that both men should hang. After the sentencing, Sheriff McCallum took Bell directly to the penitentiary.[324] Hoffman would stay in the Otoe County jail.

David Hoffman was born on April 8, 1863 into a large family near Mount Pleasant, Iowa. He had eight siblings, which included four sisters and four brothers. Hoffman left home at the age of 13 and began consorting with tramps and petty criminals. Since he never attended a day of school, he was illiterate, but had the ability to live by his wits. Between working odd jobs and stealing, he survived on his own for over 10 years. Some of Hoffman's stints were with the railroads; providing him with the familiarity of their operation.[325] Hoffman's steadiest railroad job was as a brakeman for the Chicago, Burlington, and Quincy railroad.[326]

John and Jennie Hoffman, David's brother and sister-in-law, were among the only relatives that visited the Otoe County jail during the two months between the trial and scheduled execution. David's parents, who had moved to Decatur County in Kansas, declined to make the 300 mile trip to see their son. His brother, Paul, who lived in Creston, Iowa, made an eleventh hour visit. His sister, Ms. Mattie Fitch, lived in Elmwood, Nebraska, and provided her brother with his strongest support. She circulated a petition in Otoe County, and gathered a large number of signatures asking Governor Thayer to commute Hoffman's sentence to life imprisonment.[327]

On July 19, 1887, Governor Thayer answered the clemency plea in a letter to Sheriff MaCallum:

71

Dear Sir: having fully considered the reasons presented in favor of a commutation of the sentence of death to imprisonment for life in the case of David Hoffman I'm constrained to inform you that I find no sufficient reason for interfering with the execution of the sentence imposed upon him by the court. The deliberate wrecking of a train and the destruction of human life is a crime so wanton and so atrocious, so cruel in planning and its results, that in my judgment, the severest penalty inflicted by the law is none too severe for all who are concerned in it.

I have been reminded that the accomplice of Hoffman in the perpetration of this fiendish deed has escaped with a comparatively light sentence. I have nothing to do with that. But the fact furnishes no justification for my relieving Hoffman of the fate that awaits him. An example must be made, with the hope that it may deter others from the commission of such deeds, and thus secure safety to the traveling public against the perpetration of such crimes. You will at once communicate my decision to the condemned man. You have your duty to perform in this case as the law directs.

Very respectfully yours

John M Thayer

The sheriff had two months to prepare for the hanging and was ready to perform his duty.[328]

On Wednesday, July 20, Mattie came to visit her brother. When she got to the jail, the sounds of the workmen putting the final touches on the gallows echoed through the halls, and she worked herself into "hysterics" by the time she reached Hoffman's cell. The siblings were allowed to hug each other, and in a short time, both were composed. Later that day, David's brothers, John and Paul, paid a lengthy visit.[329]

The Rev. R. Pearson was Hoffman's spiritual advisor and earlier in the week had baptized him. On Thursday evening, he and Hoffman talked until nearly 10:30 P. M. Hoffman awoke early the next morning and ate a big breakfast. At 10 A. M. on Friday, W. F. N. Houser, in the company of Sheriff McCallum, read the death warrant to Hoffman. The warrant stipulated that, "between the hours of 9 o'clock in the forenoon and 3 o'clock in the afternoon, of said day, you be hanged by the neck until you are dead, and that you pay the costs of the prosecution taxed at the sum of $735.38 and execution is awarded."[330]

Hoffman was allowed to say goodbye to his three siblings, and at 10:20, in the company of Sheriff McCallum, Reverend Pearson, and Reverend Stewart, was escorted to the scaffold which had been erected next to the jail. As they stood on the gallows, Rev. Pearson prayed and then Hoffman tried to speak, but nearly collapsed and was subsequently supported by a deputy sheriff. Hoffman had previously asked the sheriff to remove his shoes before the hanging, and he was allowed to do so. Next, the sheriff adjusted the noose around his neck, placed the black cap over his head, and asked him if he had anything to say before he died. Hoffman replied, "nothing," and at that, the sheriff, "sprung the trap which launched the soul of the train wrecker into eternity." Hoffman's neck was not broken by the fall, and he eventually strangled to death. It took 8 minutes for the noose to do its job.[331]

According to reports, the National Guard was called upon to keep order among the several thousand persons who gathered outside of the jail area. Estimates of those who were actual witnesses to the hanging were 50 by one news account and 200 by another.[332] The body was taken down by Coroner Brauer and turned over to the family. A funeral procession consisting of several buggies headed for Unadilla, 13 miles west of Dunbar, where Hoffman was buried.[333]

Authorities worked quickly to remove the scaffold and perimeter fencing. A rumor circulated that there was talk of a lynching of another Otoe County jail prisoner, Lee Shellenberger, and even though the sheriff had taken steps to ensure that didn't happen, he did not want the gallows still standing to tempt a potential mob. When the remnants of the execution were totally removed, the National Guard was also released, and the sheriff felt comfortable that order would prevail in Nebraska City.[334] To his dismay, it did not, and Shellenberger was lynched that night.

James Bell, Hoffman's accomplice, was released from the Nebraska Penitentiary in May of 1894 after serving 7 years.[335]

Charles W. Seymour

David Hoffman

Nebraska City's Grand Pacific Hotel (ca. 1909)
Copyright MemorialLibrary.com

Train wreck

Judge Samuel Chapman

Sheriff McCallum

Chapter VII
Albert Haunstine
The Clairvoyant

Custer County in Nebraska was named after General George Armstrong Custer. Its county seat, Broken Bow, was dubbed with the colorful name after a broken bow was found on an old Indian hunting ground.[336] As the names suggest, the county is rich in frontier history, including infamous murders and lynchings. The list of stories is topped by the Olive gang affair, which was prompted by a feud between cattlemen and homesteaders. It included a murder, retaliation and a double lynching, and even the alleged bribery of a respected sheriff.[337] Most of the county's residents, if asked, would probably characterize the 1888 cold blooded murder of Hiram Roten and William Ashley by a German immigrant named Albert Haunstine as second on their top 10 Custer County crimes list. The incident began on November 9, 1888, but was not over until May 22, 1891.[338] There were several twists and turns along the way.

Albert Haunstine was not unlike thousands of emigrants who came from Europe and ended up homesteading on the plains of Nebraska. His family was from Germany and settled in Newark, Ohio. His brother Joseph came west and established a homestead within Grant Township in southern Custer County. Albert followed his brother, and staked out a farm near his brother. Once his farm was established, the 25 year old Haunstine took a wife, marrying 16 year old Luella Collamore, who lived in neighboring Loup County. The couple became known by many in the community in just a short period of time.[339]

Both victims, Hiram Roten and William Ashley, were local school board officials, and Roten was also a constable. Haunstine would later say that Roten was a good friend, which is debatable, but it is clear that all of the men were neighbors and did know each other. That particular fall, the local area, including the schoolhouse, was experiencing some petty thefts, and for some reason, the school officials evidently suspected Haunstine. Rumors of Haunstine's involvement circulated in the area, which prompted him to travel to Broken Bow and talk with the Custer County Attorney, Homer M. Sullivan. Haunstine would later say that he was considering legal action to stop the rumors and harassment. Sullivan's only advice to Haunstine at that time was to protect himself; however, it is unknown in what context the advice was given.[340]

On the evening of November 9, 1888, Roten and Ashley stopped by the school to check and see if it was secure. It didn't take them long to figure out something was amiss. The school had been visited by a burglar, who took several small items, including the school's clock. As the men surveyed the scene, they noticed the burglar left a clear set of wagon tracks, which were easy to follow. The two sleuths followed the trail, which led to the farm of Albert Haunstine.[341]

The two men went to Haunstine's farm with the intention of confronting him about the theft and the fact that the evidence led straight to him. They tied their horses to Haunstine's wagon and went into the house. When Haunstine was questioned, he readily admitted that he was the thief, and returned the clock to the two men. Haunstine asked both Roten and Ashley if they wanted to stay for supper, and as expected, they both refused. The two men left the house and as they were walking toward their horses Haunstine opened the door of the house. He shot Roten in the back of the head from a distance of about 15 feet, and when Ashley turned to see what was happening, he was shot in the side of the head. Both men were killed instantly. More than likely, neither man saw it coming.[342]

Haunstine went back into the house and told his young wife that he had done something bad and they had to leave right away. The couple packed a few things and then hid the two bodies. They drug them from the front of the house and, after removing all of their valuables, hid them under a hay stack. Once they had their buggy loaded, they decided to get rid of the victim's horses. The adjacent homestead was abandoned, so they took the horses to the empty barn and tied them up, leaving them without food or water. Early in the morning of November 10, 1888, Haunstine and his wife left their farm and the evidence of his crime behind.[343]

The couple traveled north, first stopping at the small town of Arnold in Custer County. They waited until nightfall before moving east away from Custer County. They slept in the prairie during the day and traveled at night. The fugitives made their way to Madison, Nebraska, which is about 175 miles east of Arnold. Haunstine found work husking corn, and worked for about three days. He sold their buggy and team of horses, and put his wife on the train for Columbus, Nebraska, which is about 30 miles to the south of Madison. Haunstine felt that if they were being sought by authorities, there would be less chance of capture if they traveled alone.[344]

It was nearly three days after the murder before friends of the missing school men made the gruesome discovery at the Haunstine farm. The bodies were badly decomposed and partially eaten by the hogs. Authorities determined the men were murdered based upon discernible bullet wounds to their heads.[345] Custer County Sheriff Charles Penn quickly concluded that the Haunstine's were nowhere to be found, and to him at least, it was evident that Haunstine was a murderer. Sheriff Penn also believed that Haunstine's wife was, more than likely, somehow complicit in the crime. Based upon his assumption, Sheriff Penn offered a $300.00 reward for Haunstine, dead or alive, and $25 to anyone providing information which led to his capture.[346]

Sheriff Penn had wanted posters printed and distributed them throughout Nebraska. The leaflets described both Haunstine and his wife, and noted the additional $400.00 offered by the State for their capture. It wasn't long before the notices paid off. On Thursday, November 22, 1888, Platte County Sheriff Martin C. Bloedorn received a telegram that Haunstine was on a train headed for Columbus. He and Columbus police officer C. M. Taylor boarded the train as soon as it arrived, and began searching for Haunstine. The two lawmen quickly found Haunstine, and Sheriff Bloedorn immediately grabbed Haunstine around the chest as Haunstine reached for a revolver he had tucked in his waistband. In addition to the revolver, Haunstine was carrying a Winchester rifle in his other hand. The sheriff and officer Taylor placed Haunstine in custody, but only after they disarmed him of another navy pistol and full cartridge belt. They took Haunstine to the Platte County jail and notified Sheriff Penn that they had his man. It wasn't long before they located Mrs. Haunstine, who had preceded her husband to Columbus, and she was also taken into custody.[347]

On Saturday the 24th of November, Sheriff Penn brought the Haunstines back to Custer County. Mrs. Haunstine was allowed to travel back with her father by buggy. At 11:00 P. M. that evening, Albert Haunstine appeared before County Court Judge John Reese and waived his preliminary examination. He was bound over for trial, which was scheduled for the following session in February. The sheriff knew that sentiment was high and decided to take Haunstine to the Nebraska State Penitentiary in Lincoln for safekeeping. He did not want Haunstine to be lynched.[348] Mrs. Haunstine was originally arrested on a charge of being an accessory to the crime. She also appeared before Judge Reese and essentially testified as to what happened at the farm and their flight. She denied having any part in the killing of Roten and Ashley, and was released to the custody of her father.[349]

On December 20, 1888, Haunstine's attorney, N. V. Harlan, filed a motion to quash his indictment based upon the fact that at the time he waived his preliminary examination, he did not know that he was being charged with 1st degree murder.[350] The court ruled against him, and the trial of Albert Haunstine began on March 20, 1889, before Judge Francis Hamer. Hamer was a veteran in terms of presiding over murder trials, including the Jim Reynolds double murder case. His no nonsense approach and experience in conducting difficult trials was well known. The State's case would have normally been prosecuted by Custer County Attorney Homer M. Sullivan, but because of his prior conversations with Haunstine and advice given to him about the victims before the murders, he was compelled to recuse himself. Retired Judge Aaron Wall was hired to prosecute Haunstine. The defense team was headed by Charles L. Gutterson, who was assisted by attorneys A. R. Humphrey and N. V. Harlen.[351]

Haunstine's trial lasted only 3 days. Judge Wall established a strong circumstantial case before introducing the fact that Haunstine had made several jail house confessions. Haunstine's defense team was kept busy trying to refute the confessions. Haunstine explained the confessions as being idle talk and bragging. Haunstine then turned his defense to the victims and said that they had been harassing him long before the incident. He said they poisoned some of the water on his homestead and his horses drank the water, making them sick. He then brought up the fact that they were the ones who were spreading the rumors that he was the area burglar, and in effect, he was only defending himself. The jury didn't believe him. He was convicted of two counts of 1st degree murder and sentenced him to hang on October 6, 1889.[352]

Haunstine's attorneys were able to halt his execution by appealing his case to the Nebraska Supreme Court. The attorneys made two arguments on Haunstine's behalf. They based the first argument on Judge Hamer's pre-trial ruling concerning his waiver of his original hearing, and the second argument was that the evidence presented at trial was not sufficient to sustain a first degree murder charge. They based the latter argument on the fact that since the incident happened after an altercation, there was insufficient time for Haunstine to premeditate the act. They asked the court to consider reducing his sentence to life in prison. The Court's answer was, "The killing was not done in the heat of passion, but was a cold-blooded, deliberate murder." The ruling, issued on January 2, 1891, affirmed the lower court's decision, which essentially paved the way for Haunstine's execution. The court sent the case back to the lower court, and the execution date was set for April 17, 1891.[353]

Haunstine was moved from the Nebraska Penitentiary in early 1891 to the new Custer County courthouse and jail at Broken Bow. The county also had a new sheriff in the person of James B. Jones, or as he was known, "Big Jim Jones." During the months preceding his date with the executioner, Haunstine began exhibiting stoic behavior which many, including the sheriff, believe was an attempt to avoid his rendezvous with the gallows. The sheriff shared his concerns with Judge Hamer, who decided that a trial to determine the condemned man's sanity was obligatory and set April 14, 1891, three days before the hanging date.[354]

The sanity hearing was conducted by the new county attorney, Mr. E. P. Campbell, and Judge Wall before Judge Hamer in the same manner as a jury trial. Members of the jury heard testimony from witnesses for the state, including Dr. Carter, physician at the state penitentiary; Dr. Knapp, superintendent of the insane asylum at Lincoln, and Dr. J. J. Pickett, county physician. Each testified that they thought Haunstine was feigning his illness. Homer Sullivan, no longer county attorney, was added to the defense team. Their witnesses consisted of Dr. Talbot, Miss Anna Crawford, Mrs. William Blair, and several others, most of whom belonged to the Nebraska Woman Suffrage Association and or the Woman's Christian Temperance Union. In terms of Haunstine's sanity, their testimony was of little value. At 1 A. M. on the morning of April 17, 1891, the jury returned their verdict and found Haunstine sane. It had been the only thing standing in the way of the execution. All the arrangements were made, and everything was in place for Haunstine's big send off. Sheriff Jones had obtained a gallows from Hall County and the perimeter fencing was put into place. It was just a question of waiting for the appointed hour.[355]

But the hour didn't come, at least on the 17th of April. Governor Boyd sent a telegram to Sheriff Jones granting

Haunstine a 30 day reprieve. The Governor did so under the mistaken belief that the sanity adjudication process was not yet complete, and was told that the reprieve was needed to stop the execution. The effect upon the citizens of Custer County and many others who were gathered to see the spectacle was disappointment. The crowd mulled around for several hours waiting to find out if the Governor would rescind the stay. Around 4 P.M., they realized that was not to be the case, and the hanging was postponed. Then the frustration turned to anger. Spectators quickly turned into a mob, and didn't want to wait to see justice done. Several hundred men began moving towards the courthouse and the jail that housed the prisoner. Many were carrying crowbars and sledge hammers, and Sheriff Jones knew exactly how dangerous the situation was and what was about to happen. Suddenly, Judge Hamer stood on the steps and began talking to the prospective vigilantes. The judge, Sheriff Jones, and several friends of the victims were eventually able to calm the crowd and get them to disperse. Thanks to them, Haunstine got his extension.[356]

The new date for Haunstine's execution was set for Friday May 22, 1891. Knowing exactly the date of his impending death was a literal epiphany for Haunstine. During the days before his scheduled execution, Haunstine spend most of his time reading scripture and praying. Apparently, he did not consider himself a member of an organized religion, and used the time to shop around for one. He requested visits by Broken Bow ministers Rev. Mr. Sayers, Rev. L. R. Beebe, and Rev. M. Shepherd. Each of them represented a separate religious denomination. He eventually asked for Father Healy, a Catholic priest who provided him a crash course in Catholicism. Just before the date of the hanging, Father Healy baptized him as a Catholic and administered the sacraments, including confession.[357]

Haunstine's transformation from insane stoic to "Hail Fellow Well Met," moved at breakneck speed. Sheriff Big Jim Jones said that before the 17th of April, he would have been able to hang Haunstine and "not flinch a bit," but he continued, "he has become so good natured and everybody has become so attached to him that I wish someone would handle him."[358] Haunstine became so amenable that he invited a reporter from *The Omaha Daily Bee* to visit him and report his verbatim confession. The newsman accommodated him and sat in his cell listening intensely to Haunstine's story. For the most part, Haunstine told the same tale residents of Broken Bow had heard over and over, but again tried to mitigate his actions by saying he was bullied into the act.[359]

Besides his new found congeniality, Haunstine demonstrated a great deal of nerve, according to Big Jim Jones, but more than likely, it was simply his acceptance of the inevitable. He told the sheriff that his only concern was that the rope might break. He also asked the sheriff if he could attach a 50 pound bag of sand to his feet to ensure that his neck would snap. The sheriff assured him that the rope would not break and there would be no need to add any additional weight. What Big Jim neglected to tell him was that he bought a special strength $12 silk rope and tested it on the morning of April 17, the date of Haunstine's reprieve. The sheriff attached it to a sandbag, and when he dropped it through the trap, it snapped. It was then that he determined that fancy was not practical. Sheriff Jones bought a traditional hemp rope, which was the tried and true tool of the frontier hangman. He then tested the new rope using a 200 pound sandbag, and it held fast both times it went through the trap door. After the test, the sheriff was not worried in the least about his promise to Haunstine.[360]

As the days in May of 1891 began to tick off, so did Haunstine's last days on earth. Sheriff Jones re-issued passes to the hanging, and made sure, as he did in April, that all the arrangements were in place for a successful execution. Meanwhile, Haunstine's visits from the Temperance League became more frequent, and his daily meditation increased exponentially. Haunstine said that he was happier than he had been in 4 years, and was confident that his sins had been forgiven.[361] On May 21, the day before the scheduled hanging, he was visited the final time by his brother and two sisters.[362]

On the morning of the hanging, an estimated crowd of 2,500 people gathered near the courthouse. At 12:30, the ticketed spectators were allowed inside of the perimeter. A relative of Hiram Roten, one of the victims, walked onto the scaffold. He tossed a block of wood over the fence as a signal that the hanging was imminent, and it was time for those who were not admitted to tear down the fence. Within minutes the fence was no longer standing, and the crowd moved towards the gallows. Sheriff Jones addressed the crowd and told them that they had broken the law, but if they agreed to stand back he would proceed with the execution. The sheriff asked the nearly silent crowd for a show of hands of those who would agree to stay back from the scaffold. Everyone raised their hand.[363]

At 12:45, Sheriff Jones went back to the jail, and read the death warrant to Haunstine. Haunstine, with Fathers Healy and Wolf on one arm and the sheriff on the other, was led into the courthouse yard and ascended the scaffold. He was clean shaven and wore a dark blue suit with a tie. He also wore a rosary around his neck, a symbol of his newly found religion. Father Healy held a crucifix to his lips while Haunstine and the two priests prayed. Albert was asked if he had anything to say, and he made a brief statement asking the onlookers for forgiveness and saying he was sorry for the trouble he had caused. When he finished, he stepped back onto the trap door. Sheriff Wilson of Buffalo County, along with some of the other visiting sheriffs, strapped his hands, legs, and ankles, while a deputy pinioned his arms. Sheriff Jones placed the noose around his neck, making sure the knot was behind his left ear, and then put the black cap over his head, securing it from behind. At 1:01 PM, the sheriff stepped back, and with a razor, cut the rope holding the trap door. What happened next shocked everyone, especially Sheriff Jones. Haunstine hit the ground "like a log." The rope had snapped, "like a piece of twine." Big Jim and the other attending sheriffs rushed to the fallen Haunstine and carried him back up to the platform. The two pieces of rope were quickly spliced back together. Haunstine, who was able to speak, begged the sheriff to loosen the rope from his neck. Even if he wanted to oblige him, the rope was cinched too tight from the jerk, and the sheriff declined. The others worked feverishly, and within minutes, at 1:04 PM, Haunstine was dropped a second time.[364]

Dr. C. H. Morris of Broken Bow and Aurora physician W. F. Goodwin, two of the attending physicians, pronounced Albert Haunstine dead at 1:10 PM. It was apparent that all in attendance did not accept Haunstine's apology. As the crowd stood and looked at his body dangling under the gallows, one of the spectators was seen spitting on him. After a short time, Haunstine's body was cut down and taken to the sheriff's office. A short service was conducted by Fathers Healy and Wolf, and he was turned over to his brother, whose intention was to bury him on his farm located 45 miles from Broken Bow.[365]

There is somewhat of a mystery surrounding the events of that Friday afternoon. Many speculated that Big Jim's rope had been tampered with when he left it unattended. Some said, but it was never proven, that friends of Roten and Ashley felt that justice would be better served if the rope broke and Haunstine had to be hung twice. After all, there were two murders, why not two hangings.[366]

Albert E. Haunstine

Sheriff Charles Penn

Albert Haunstine Execution - May 22, 1891
Original Courtesy Nebraska State Historical Society

Chapter VIII
Christian Furst and Charles Shepard
Incipient Idiots

In 1921, Crowell, Nebraska was described as, "a small village on the line of the old Fremont, Elkhorn & Missouri Valley Railroad (now Chicago & Northwestern system), in Pebble Township."[367] Crowell was located in western Dodge County. In 1873, a post office and a railroad station were established in Crowell. In the autumn of 1883, "J. J. King came from Fremont and erected a frame store building and placed on sale a stock of general merchandise." Also that year, J. L. Baker built a grain warehouse. In 1884, Fred Mundt opened a general store, James Cusick a livery stable, John B. Taylor a hardware store, John Harmal a blacksmith shop, Herman Diers a hotel, and Carlos Pulsifer established a granary.[368] Today, the only evidence that the village ever existed is the small cemetery just to the southeast of the now defunct Crowell. There are but 70 souls perpetually resting in the small cemetery. The most famous resident is Carlos True Pulsifer.

Carl Pulsifer was born in New Hampshire in 1835. His brother Frank was born in 1839. Carl was described as rough and rugged, and was well-liked and respected by most in the Crowell community.[369] Carl, along with his younger brother Frank, served in Company A of the 5th Regiment Iowa Cavalry during the Civil War. Company A was part of the regiment organized in Omaha, Nebraska in the fall of 1861, and saw plenty of action before war's end.[370] By the late 1880s, both Carl and Frank were well settled residents of the small village of Crowell in Dodge County. Carl and his wife, Kate, with their eight children lived about ½ mile west of town. Carl dabbled in coal, lumber, and grain trading before establishing the Crowell granary.

On the night of December 10, 1889, Carl closed his granary, just as he did every evening, and began the half mile trek over the railroad tracks to his home. There was a rumor in the small community that because Crowell had no bank, Pulsifer always carried the daily business receipts home with him at night. The stories went further by adding that he always carried a large sum of money.[371]

Charles Shepard was a 20 year old man who also lived in the Crowell area. He had some training in the art of smithy, but was a long way from becoming a blacksmith. He mostly worked in the livery stable cleaning up. Charles had a 20 year old friend named Christian Furst, who lived a few miles south in Scribner, Nebraska.[372] Furst, like Shepard, had not as yet established a salable vocation and was having trouble holding down a job. He also was an inspiring blacksmith and worked on and off in a shop in Scribner. It was the misfortune of Carl Pulsifer that neither Furst nor Shepard was an accomplished highwayman. The two men hatched a plot to waylay Carl on his way home and steal his money. Their plan was in trouble from the beginning.[373]

The two men armed themselves with two pistols. One carried a long .38 caliber revolver and the other a regular .32. About dusk, the two hid themselves inside a culvert, which ran under the railroad tracks near where Carl normally crossed the tracks. They waited until about 6:20 P.M., when they saw a figure walking towards them carrying a lantern. They knew right away that it was their intended victim Pulsifer. During the winter, he always carried a lantern to help him light his way. As he was about to cross the tracks, Shepard and Furst ran from the culvert and accosted Pulsifer. They told him to raise his hands, but, purportedly, instead he reached in his pocket. Both men each fired two shots at Carl, one of them striking him in the chest. It passed directly through his heart, killing him instantly.[374]

The bandits quickly went through the pockets of their victim, looking for the prize, but it wasn't there. They took the small amount of money he had on his person, a pocketbook, and some other papers and fled. For most, it's hard to understand the quiet that must have existed at that time, long before such things as radio or television. The reports of the pistols were so loud they were heard by most everyone in the village. Carl's 19 year old son, John, was at home waiting for his father when the shots rang out. He looked towards the direction of the volleys and saw the light from his father's lantern grow dim and then go dark. He rushed to the scene and found Carl on the ground, bleeding profusely and unresponsive. John Pulsifer's dad was dead.[375]

The two bungling outlaws began their escape by running from the scene on foot. Several witnesses saw the figures of two men as they fled. The pair made their way through farm fields, and as they ran, they tossed Pulsifer's pocketbook into a field. They stopped just long enough to hide his ledger under a haystack. They headed west until they reached the Shoemaker farm, where they stopped and bought a loaf of bread. They then turned north and headed for West Point, Nebraska, which was about 10 miles north of Crowell.[376] When they finally reached West Point, the two did what any two fledgling hoodlums would do; they took refuge in "the sporting house of Jenny Burns."[377]

Meanwhile, the news of the shooting spread quickly through Crowell and Scribner, and before long, a makeshift posse of 100 men began searching the area. It was obvious to them that the two suspects were on foot, and a diligent search should produce the murderers. Dodge County Sheriff James P. Mallon headed the hunt, and quickly established a reward for the fugitives. Carl's brother Frank Pulsifer put up $1,000, the governor $500, and the sheriff $400. Within a day, there was a $1,900 price on the heads of the two suspects. During the search, the identity of the two figures seen running in the dark became clear. W. A. Connolly, the owner of restaurant in Scribner, saw Shepard and Furst the day of the murder, walking in the alley behind the restaurant. The two had approached a doctor in town on the afternoon of the murder and asked if they could borrow a revolver from him. The doctor refused them, but the story also put the pair together the day of the murder. Two other witnesses saw them walking on the railroad tracks from Scribner towards Crowell around 4 P.M. on the same day. The sheriff assembled the information, and because both men were conspicuously absent from their normal haunts, he was relatively sure he knew who killed Carl Pulsifer.[378]

On December 12, two days after the murder, both Shepard and Furst rode into Crowell on two stolen horses. The men had taken a team of horses at West Point and decided to go south. It was evident that the stolen horses were not in the best condition. For that reason, they headed back through Crowell with the thought that they could steal a better team in Scribner. It didn't take long for the pair to find out that everyone within 25 miles was looking for them. Both men lit out on foot and headed for the Elkhorn River. The two were quickly caught and gave up without a fight. Josh King, the owner of a general store in Crowell, led several men and arrested Shepard. George Bowlus and another group of men captured Furst just shortly after the apprehension of Shepard.[379]

Josh King took Shepard back to his store and held him there until it was decided what to do with the pair. Shepard began talking to King, and he immediately confessed to shooting

Pulsifer. He told King that they shot him when he refused to "throw up," meaning raise his hands. After their conversation, King put Shepard in his buggy and headed for Scribner. George Bowlus and some of the others took Furst, keeping the two separated. Once the suspects were at Scribner, Furst was taken to the jail and King took Shepard to the Clifton House hotel and waited for the sheriff to arrive. King would later testify that Shepard talked to him during the buggy ride and once again repeated the story when they were at the hotel.[380] Sheriff Mallon arrived in Scribner sometime after noon and took charge of the prisoners. A crowd of nearly 500 men seriously considered lynching the pair, but the sheriff amassed a group of 30 armed deputies to ensure that the suspects got out of town safely. Between a group of cool headed men from Scribner and the armed deputies, the sheriff and the two suspects were able to board the 2:40 train to Fremont, the county seat. After arriving in Fremont, Shepard and Furst were safely placed in jail.[381]

As soon as Charles Shepard and Christian Furst were incarcerated, they began a second series of confessions. Each confession was not only an acknowledgement, but changed just slightly in an attempt to mitigate their crime. They both would say that they only opened fire on Pulsifer when instead of raising his hands, he reached in his pocket and they thought he was reaching for a pistol. Both men signed written confessions.[382] Shepard and Furst were indicted for first degree murder, and subsequently filed affidavits to the court indicating they were indigent.[383] The court appointed Thomas M. Franse of West Point to represent Shepard and Conrad Hollenbeck of Fremont to represent Furst.[384]

On December 13, 1889, after meeting with this client, Attorney Thomas Franse contacted Sheriff Mallon and said his client had something important to tell him. Franse told the sheriff that his client and Furst were hired to kill Pulsifer by Herman Diers. Diers, incidentally, was the foreman of the coroner's jury that held the inquest in the death of Pulsifer just a day before. Sheriff Mallon then checked with others, including Frank Pulsifer, and found out that there may have been bad blood between the two Crowell business men. It was relayed to the sheriff that at one point in time, Carl Pulsifer told his brother if anything ever happened to him, it was Diers who was responsible.[385] Armed with this information, the sheriff located Diers on a train the following Sunday and placed him under arrest and placed him in the county jail. The bad blood, if there really was any, was well known to everyone in Crowell including Charles Shepard. Herman Diers was released within a few days without charges being filed.[386]

The trial of Charles Shepard and Christian Furst began on January 27, 1890, with Judge William Marshall presiding. The state was represented by Dodge County Attorney George L. Loomis. The first order of business for Attorneys Franse and Hollenbeck was to offer a motion to separate the two defendants. Judge Marshall agreed and decided that Shepard would be tried first. The selection of a jury did not go well, and Judge Marshall sent the sheriff into the county with orders to find more potential jurors. It took two entire days to seat a jury and hear opening arguments.[387]

The state called several witnesses who testified to a series of events that seemingly proved a strong circumstantial case against Shepard. The testimony included the finding of Pulsifer's pocketbook and ledger book where Shepard said they would be found. Both Shepard and Furst were linked to a discarded revolver and two others purportedly used to kill Pulsifer. Josh King testified about Shepard's arrest, his trip to Scribner, and the time he spent at the hotel waiting for Sheriff Mallon. The major impact of King's testimony was the re-telling of Shepard's confessions. Courtroom spectators became engrossed and listened intensely to King's every word. The silence was disrupted by a low murmur when Mr. King disclosed that the total amount of proceeds from the crime was $19 in cash. Mr. Loomis also was able to enter a written confession made by Shepard after he was jailed in Fremont.[388] Loomis rested the state's case at 10:30 A.M.

Shepard's defense was weak. Dr. Sommers offered testimony concerning his mental stability. William Shepherd, the father of Charles, also testified that his son had become unstable. Franse continued this strategy by saying that the young Shepard was "undermined," both physically and mentally by his father, which ultimately created not insanity, but "incipient idiocy," in his client.[389] Mr. Franse then turned to a more significant argument. His assertion was that each confession made by his client was done while he was under duress and should not be considered. Next, Shepard took the witness stand and asserted that he shot Pulsifer, but it was in self-defense.[390]

George Loomis made a strong closing argument, and Mr. Franse based his final plea on trying to save his client's life. He repeated that Shepard was mentally unstable and that the confessions obtained from him were coerced. Based upon these facts, he argued that the jury should consider a charge of murder in the second degree for his client. Judge Marshall provided the jury with instructions and sent them to deliberate around 6:00 P.M. It took the jury 3 hours and 50 minutes to reach a unanimous decision. After a long 6 day trial, the jury found Charles Shepard guilty of murder in the first degree.[391] Shepard showed no emotion when the verdict was read. As was expected, Judge Marshall was asked to consider a new trial for Shepard. During the second week of March, just before the beginning of the Furst trial, Judge Marshall denied Shepard's request, and sentenced him to hang on June 13, 1890.[392]

March 17, 1890, was St. Patrick's Day and the beginning of Christian Furst's murder case. Like the Charles Shepard trial, it was difficult to find jurors who had not as yet formed an opinion, and a second pool had to be drawn. A second day came and went with the exhaustion of the second pool. It took an unprecedented 3 days to simply seat the jury.[393] John Pulsifer was one of the first witnesses to testify. He told of finding his father's body after he rushed to the scene of the shooting. Dr. Sommers, who assisted at the autopsy, described Pulsifer's fatal wounds. The testimony continued a second day with essentially the same witnesses and same testimony as was provided at the Shepard trial. An intimate of Jenny Burns' sporting house in West Point, Miss Richmond, identified Furst as being at the establishment the day after the murder. Also, as in the Shepard case, the confessions elicited by Mr. Bowlus, who arrested and transported Furst, became contentious before they were finally admitted. When Furst was placed in jail, he made a verbal confession. Bowlus then had Furst repeat the confession as he carefully wrote it down. After the confession was reduced to writing, Bowlus made Furst sign it. The judge eventually ruled against the admission of the written confession, but allowed Bowlus to testify to the rendition of its contents.[394]

Mr. Hollenbeck presented a similar defense as did Mr. Franse in terms of his client's mental capacity to commit first degree murder. He used medical experts, in the persons of Dr. DeVries and Dr. Abbott, who first established the fact that the act of suicide is only committed by a person who is insane. Next, he introduced the fact that three years prior to the murder, Furst's father committed suicide, and therefore, Christian should also be considered as being of unsound mind.[395] That was the extent of Mr. Hollenbeck's defense.

In the late afternoon of March 25, 1890, summations were presented and the judge instructed the jury. They were given the case at 6:00 P.M. At 10:00 P.M., the courtroom was still filled with persons milling around waiting for the jury to come back. At 10:30, their patience paid off. The defendant was brought from the jail and he and his attorney sat tolerantly waiting to hear the results.[396] "We the jury being duly impaneled and sworn in the above entitled cause find the defendant Christian Furst guilty of murder in the first degree in manner and form as charged in the indictment."[397] Christian Furst, just like Charles Shepard, showed no emotion when hearing the verdict.[398] Mr. Hollenbeck, as standard protocol, asked the court for a new trial for his client. On April 14, 1890, Judge Marshall answered the plea and denied it. Judge Marshall then sentenced Christian Furst to hang on July 25, 1890.[399]

Thomas Franse, the attorney for Charles Shepard, and Conrad Hollenbeck, Furst's attorney, both filed appeals to the Nebraska Supreme Court. Shepard's argument, in essence, was that the ruling on the admissibility of his confessions was wrong. Franse also asked in his appeal that the court, based upon the evidence presented, reduce the conviction to second degree murder. Hollenbeck posed a similar argument concerning the confessions, but also that the court should have seriously considered the insanity defense posed to the district court. Lastly, as did Franse, he asked that the court view the evidence to see if a conviction for second degree murder might have been more appropriate.[400]

On February 17, 1891, the Nebraska Supreme Court issued rulings on both cases. In the Shepard appeal, they said that the confessions made after the men were in jail were not made under duress and therefore admissible. The court also ruled on the evidence and said, "the evidence fully sustains the verdict of murder in the first degree. Under the testimony, no other verdict could have properly been returned. The judgment is affirmed."[401] In Furst's appeal, the court said the same thing concerning the admissibility of the confession, and also the court ruled that the trial judge's instruction to the jury on the issue of insanity was proper. Lastly, the court ruled on the evidence presented and said, "There is in the record no evidence which would warrant us in reducing the sentence. The defendant is either guilty of murder in the first degree or he is innocent. The testimony fully warranted the jury in finding that the defendant was sane, and that he and Sheppard murdered Pulsifer in attempting to rob him. The defendant was accorded a fair and impartial trial. The judgment of the district court is affirmed."[402] The Supreme Court set the execution date for both Shepard and Furst as June 5, 1891.[403]

When the Supreme Court denied the appeals of both men, it became the duty of Sheriff Mallon to prepare for the execution, but not for long. On April 24, 1891, Sheriff James Mallon resigned his post as Dodge County Sheriff to become the warden of Nebraska's penitentiary.[404] Governor Boyd's appointment lifted the burden from Mallon's shoulders; however, it created a problem for the Dodge County Board of Supervisors. Their job was to find a new sheriff, and to make things worse, the Board had just taken a three month hiatus. They realized that anyone applying for the job would inherit the unenviable task of executing two young men. The Board quickly pushed forward, however, and conducted a diligent search. Luckily, they found James Milliken. He agreed to take the job and was appointed at a special session of the supervisors during the first week of May, 1891, which was less than a month before the execution date.[405]

The new sheriff faced several problems as he began preparing for the hanging. The impending double execution, for example, was the first of its kind in the state. History also helped him to understand that very few of the previous executions in the state went off as planned. Unruly crowds were the rule rather than the exception. To make matters worse, with only two weeks to go before the date of the hanging, Custer County hung Albert Haunstine in Broken Bow. The botched hanging only exacerbated Sheriff Milliken's concerns. He knew that the presence of the National Guard would make little difference if and when the mob decided they wanted a view of the proceedings.[406]

Meanwhile, while the sheriff made preparations for the execution, a large number of persons in Dodge County circulated petitions to the governor asking for clemency for the 21 year olds Shepard and Furst. The majority of signers were opposed to capital punishment, but others were friends of the men's families. Many believed that, although similar clemency efforts had failed in the past, the age of the men may have greater significance in terms of the governor's decision. It was rumored that Sheriff Milliken was one such person.[407]

The Dodge County Jail was located in a separate building just to the south of the courthouse. The building was constructed in the style of Second Empire architecture, with a mansard roof and hooded dormer windows."[408] The sheriff consulted the Nebraska Statue which said,"...such punishment shall be inflicted in the immediate vicinity of the jail, within an enclosure to be prepared for that purpose under the direction of the sheriff, which enclosure shall be higher than the gallows, and so constructed as to exclude the view of persons outside thereof."[409] Based upon his reading, Sheriff Milliken decided to have the gallows constructed on the inside of the jail. The architecture of the jail would accommodate a gallows, and also greatly enhance the security surrounding the event.[410]

Adding to the confusion of Dodge County needing a new sheriff, was the uncertainty of who would decide the issue of clemency. Governor John Thayer was defeated by James Boyd in the governor's race. Thayer sued Boyd, challenging the qualification of his citizenship. The state courts reversed the election and gave the job back to Thayer. Boyd filed suit in the United States Supreme Court, and the prior rulings were reversed and Boyd got his job back. In the case of Shepard and Furst, Governor Thayer was called upon to decide. He sent his answers in person with his son, John Thayer, who traveled to Fremont by train and hand delivered the governor's answers the day before the scheduled hanging. The first letter was to Sheriff Milliken and the second was for the attorneys for the condemned men.[411]

To Sheriff Milliken, the Governor wrote: "Having given most careful and thoughtful consideration to the cases of Charles E Shepherd and Christian Furst, I have come to the conclusion that I cannot interfere with the execution of the sentence which was imposed upon them by the court. And the performance of your most painful duty, I trust you will be amply prepared with the proper appliances." To the Attorneys: "After a careful and thorough consideration of all cases of Charles E Shepherd and Christian Furst, I have come to the conclusion that is not my duty to interfere with the sentence imposed upon them. I trust you will make this known to the parents and brothers and sisters of Shepherd so they can avail themselves of the intervening time to visit their son and brother." Both letters were signed by Governor Thayer.[412]

On the morning of June 5, 1891, Sheriff Milliken had completed the necessary arrangements for the hanging. The relatively small space limited the number of spectators. The space allocated was only for 18 or 19 persons. The sheriff anticipated the attendance as being his staff, a few visiting sheriffs, a few credentialed news media, the clergy, Shepard's family, Furst's family, and Pulsifer's brother and son.[413]

At 10:20 A. M. on June 5, 1891, Sheriff Milliken entered the cell where Shepard and Furst were in consultation with Reverend Harrison of Scribner, who was the spiritual advisor to the men. Reverend Harrison stepped out into the hall as the sheriff read the death warrants. Neither man seemed affected by the reading. Furst asked Milliken how long before they made the trip to the gallows and the sheriff told them they had 20 minutes. Both men were neatly attired in new dark suits and ties. Shepard wore a white rose in his lapel and Furst a red rose. The crowd of onlookers consisted of reporters from the Fremont and *Omaha Bee* newspapers, 8 other county sheriffs, 3 officials from the state penitentiary, 4 officers from the Omaha Police Department, and 4 physicians. The families of the condemned men visited them the night before and were not in attendance.[414]

The men walked up the steps of the gallows. Furst took his place on the south trap door, while Shepard stood on the north one. Each man was able to look out of a window directly in front of them. As they stood there contemplating their fate, they watched and listened to a heavy downpour of rain. Each was asked if they had anything to say, and Furst replied, "I haven't anything to say." Shepard replied, "we're the men who did the deed, and justly being punished for the crime and therefore no one can be accused of it." Some believed that it was Shepard's way of apologizing to Herman Diers for trying to shift the blame onto him. The sheriff and his men quickly moved to strap the arms and legs of the two men. As soon as they finished, the black caps were placed over their heads. Next the sheriff placed a noose around each man's neck and adjusted it so the knot was behind the left ear. From under the black hood, Shepard said, "please put it down, it hurts me." Sheriff Milliken then re-adjusted the noose and stepped backwards while looking at the placement of Furst's noose. While the crowd watched his apparent perusal of the knots, he pulled the lever and both men dropped.[415]

Both men's necks were snapped, and the spectators seemed to breathe a sigh of relief that the ropes held. Furst did not move, and Shepard's convulsions were short in duration. Dr. DeVries, the acting coroner, with the assistance of the other physicians, monitored the vital signs of both men. Furst was declared dead after 14 minutes and Shepard 19. The bodies were left hanging for 25 minutes, then cut down, placed in coffins, and taken to the "embalming parlor." Furst's remains were given to his parents for burial in Fremont, and Shepard was taken to Crowell for burial.[416]

In December of 1890, Herman Diers filed a civil suit against Sheriff Mallon and another against Frank Pulsifer on charges of false arrest. The case went before a jury and lasted until 1892, when the suit was eventually dismissed.[417] There was little doubt, however, that the bad blood between Pulsifer and Diers never went further than a few angry words.

Carlos T. Pulsifer

Herman Diers

Charles Shepard

Christian Furst

Dodge County Courthouse with County Jail Building on Left (ca. 1900)

Manhattan Cemetery - Dodge County

Chapter IX
Ed Neal or Ed Neil
The Death Machine

"The death machine" was described in great detail in the October 10, 1891 Saturday Edition of the *Omaha Daily Bee* newspaper. "The scaffold was built of pine and in a most enduring manner. The floor was of two-inch planks, the supporting posts being nine inches square. The joists were two inches in thickness and six inches wide. They were firmly fastened with large bolts to the corner posts. Upon them the floor rested, the planks being made secure by heavy spikes. The cross piece from which the rope descended was a heavy timber six inches square. It was supported at either end by uprights which are 14 feet high. The rope drops through a hole in the cross piece directly over the trap.

The latter was three feet square. One end was fastened to the floor of the scaffold by a stout pair of iron hinges. The boards of the trap ran crosswise to those of the floor and were bound together by heavy cleats screwed to all the pieces. At the end of the cleat farthest from the braces there was a heavy iron staple about five inches in height. This was securely fastened to the cleats and extended through a hole in the floor from beneath. Into the staple was inserted a large wooden wedge. The wedge supported the trap on the same plane as the floor. When removed the trap would fall and maintain a perpendicular position beneath the gallows. The wedge ran in a groove in which a plunger worked. The latter was controlled by a lever on the right hand side of the platform. By pulling the lever back, the plunger was shot forward along the slot until the wedge gave way before it, thus removing the support and allowing trap to fall."[418]

The need for the building of this particular "death machine" can be traced to sometime shortly after 3:00 P.M. on the 3rd of February, 1890. That's the last time Allen and Dorothy Jones were seen alive. The last place they were seen was at a farm owned by Dr. Pinney, a resident of Council Bluffs, Iowa.[419] Dr. Pinney's farmstead was described at the time as being southwest of Omaha, adjacent to Seymour Park. Today the area is a town of

6,000 people known as the City of Ralston, Nebraska. Ralston is surrounded by Omaha on three sides and Sarpy County on the other.[420]

The circumstances that brought the couple to the Pinney farm began when Dr. Pinney made arrangements to lease the farm to a man named A. B. Cadwalader, who also lived near Council Bluffs, Iowa. Cadwalader was unable to take possession of the farm at the time of the agreement. He persuaded his elderly in-laws, Allen and Dorothy Jones, to stay at the farm and tend the livestock until he could make arrangements to occupy it. Allen Jones was 72 at the time and Dorothy was 60.[421] Traveling to the farm was a long trek for the elderly couple. They lived in Irvington, Nebraska, which is on the northwest outskirts of Omaha. The couple rode to the Pinney farm in a wagon pulled by two horses, a drive of approximately 12 miles, or about six hours. There were not many animals at the farm, and Cadwalader believed that his in-laws should be able to care for them with little difficulty. The livestock consisted of eight head of cows and a couple of calves. Also being kept at the farm was one more small calf, one yearling, and eight head of horses all belonging to Dr. Pinney.[422]

On February 10, 1890, Mrs. Cadwalader and her son, Ira, went to visit her parents at the Pinney farm. When they arrived they were somewhat mystified as they found no one there. They made a superficial search and discovered the livestock was missing too. Mrs. Cadwalader thought that it was possible that her parents had returned to Irvington, taking the animals with them. The interior of the house showed no unusual signs whatsoever, which supported her assumption that the couple may have just left.[423] She notified her brother, Nathan Jones, who also lived in Irvington that their parents were not at the farm. Unfortunately, in 1890, communications were limited, so she used the fastest available at that time. She sent him a letter. Mrs. Cadwalader and her son spent the night at the farm. They woke up early, had another look around, and then returned to Council Bluffs.[424] The next day, on the 12th of February, Nathan received his sister's letter. He dropped what he was doing and went to the Pinney farm and began searching. He looked for his parents in the house and the barns, but, like his sister, was unable to find even a trace of them. Nathan became worried and decided to go to Council Bluffs and talk directly with his sister. At first, Mrs. Cadwalader was surprised that her parents didn't go back to Irvington. The two siblings discussed the situation, and then notified Dr. Pinney of their missing parents and his livestock. Dr.

Pinney began thinking what was almost unthinkable for the times. He assumed the couple may have been abducted and his livestock stolen.[425]

Dr. Pinney, Nathan Jones, and a man identified as Arthur Phillips traveled back to the farm, arriving around sundown. Along the way, they asked neighbors if they had heard or seen anything of the elderly couple. No one knew or saw a thing. It was too dark to begin searching when they finally arrived, so they went to bed. When they arose early on the morning of the 13th of February, they began searching the farm in earnest. The trio was joined by other men from the area who heard about the missing couple and came to assist in the search. Two of the neighbors, Frank Selder and Henry Ruser, were the first to make the grim discovery. They found the body of Allen Jones at the bottom of a manure pile east of the barn, partially covered up with manure.[426] At that point, the search intensified and the body of Dorothy was found on the east side of the barn, hidden under a hay stack. Both Allen and Dorothy Jones apparently died of gunshot wounds. First reports from the scene showed that Allen suffered three bullet wounds to the back between the shoulder blades, and Dorothy was shot twice in the back.[427] The condition of both bodies made the discovery exceptionally gruesome. Besides the bodies undergoing the decomposition process, rats had been feeding on the faces of both victims.[428] After the bodies were removed to the undertaker's parlor, Coroner Harrigan and Dr. McManigal conducted an autopsy. Dorothy was struck on the left side of her back 4 times, and Allen had 3 bullet wounds found just under the right shoulder. Both victims were shot with a .38 cal. pistol.[429]

Douglas County Sheriff John Boyd was in-charge of the investigation. He firmly believed that the murderer was acquainted with the farm and that the motive was the theft of the livestock. Several people were brought in for questioning and some were detained. Boyd turned his efforts to finding the livestock. The investigation disclosed that a man named Ed Neal hired two men in South Omaha to go to the Pinney farm and help drive livestock back to South Omaha. Neal told the men he was tired of farming and wanted to liquidate his holdings.[430] Neal and the men returned to the farm and the stock was brought back to South Omaha, where it was all sold to the Boyer's Brothers livestock brokers.[431] Meanwhile, Omaha police detectives determined that a man named Ed Neal; a drifter from St. Joseph, Missouri, was seen in South Omaha on the 3rd of February and the following day in downtown Omaha. The witness, who saw him on the morning of the 4th of February in downtown Omaha, noted that Neal had a gun in his possession.[432]

After selling the stock, Neal went to a jewelry store in South Omaha and bought a woman's gold watch and chain and an eighteen carat gold ring. He paid for part of the purchase by trading another gold ring which at trial was identified as belonging to Dorothy Jones.[433] Neal stayed in South Omaha and also in Downtown Omaha for several days spending what appeared to be his ill-gotten gains. He subsequently went to Union Station, where he boarded the train bound for Kansas City.[434]

The Omaha Police notified the Kansas City authorities to be on the lookout for a person who may be stealing cattle in their area. They said he was also was wanted for questioning in the murder of the Jones couple. Shortly thereafter, Kansas City Police notified Omaha's Chief Seavy that they apprehended an individual for stealing cattle who matched the description of the man wanted by the Omaha police. After conducting an investigation, Kansas City authorities determined that the man in custody, Ed Neal, had pawned several of the items he purchased in both Omaha and South Omaha. Douglas County Sheriff John Boyd obtained a Governor's warrant for Neal, and subsequently extradited him back to Omaha.[435]

Neal at first denied any knowledge of Omaha or South Omaha and said he had never been in either city. Upon being confronted with the two men hired to drive the livestock to South Omaha, he then changed his story by saying that he bought the livestock from a man named Shellenberg.[436] Neal told Sheriff Boyd that he was acquainted with Shellenberg because the two men were involved in the theft of a horse in Missouri Valley, Iowa in 1888 and that both men spent time together in the Logan County jail. He told the sheriff that Shellenberg's first name was Joe, and that he lived in Nebraska City.[437]

The news that Neal had implicated Fuller aka Joe Shellenberg was widely circulated and appeared in the Omaha newspapers as well as in Nebraska City. Omaha police went to Nebraska City and found Shellenberg, who was apparently awaiting authorities. He indicated that he had nothing to do with the incident and he read that Neal named him as an accomplice. Shellenberg also said that he was not worried because he had an iron clad alibi and could prove he was not within 50 miles of the scene at the time the crime was committed.[438]

Shellenberg was placed under arrest and brought to Omaha where he was interrogated in Chief Seavy's office. He admitted knowing Neal and being an accomplice in the Missouri Valley crime. He said he had not seen Neal since they were released from jail and wasn't surprised that Neal was trying to involve him in the murder. He also said that Neal had told him that if he ever had the opportunity to get him into trouble, he would. Sheriff Boyd contacted the prosecutor in Iowa and asked about Shellenberg and Neal. His answer was that it was his opinion that if Shellenberg had anything to do with the murder, he was convinced it was "as a tool of Neal."[439]

Neal was tried at the May term of the court in 1890. On May 12, 1890, he was arraigned in Douglas County District Court before Judge Joseph R. Clarkson. He was prosecuted by Mr. Timothy J. Mahoney, Douglas County's prosecuting attorney. Neal pled not guilty, and then was asked by the judge if he "had means to employ counsel?" Neal replied that he did not, and added that Mr. William Gurley and Mr. Lee Estelle had been handling his case. Judge Clarkson ruled that the two attorneys were to continue on Neal's behalf.[440]

The trial began the day following Neal's arraignment on May 14, 1890. Neal's attorneys tried immediately to forestall the proceeding by challenging the way in which the jury was summoned, but Judge Clarkson ruled against them. The first day of the trial was spent entirely on selecting a jury from the pool. One-by-one, jurors provided reasons why they shouldn't be selected. Some that said they could be unbiased where challenged by the defense, and the judge was required to issue a call for a new group of potential jurors. The following morning, the Neal jury was finally seated. The afternoon session was taken up by opening statements.[441]

Mr. Mahoney began meticulously calling witnesses to establish that Allen and Dorothy Jones were well and alive, and all of the livestock was at the farm before their daughter discovered them missing. Witnesses described the search for the couple and then the more extensive search for their bodies. Dr. Harrigan, Douglas County's coroner, was called and testified about the postmortem exam and the cause of death. Mahoney asked Harrigan about bruising on the bodies, and he replied that he believed they were inflicted postmortem. By the second week of the trial, a strange phenomenon occurred. With each day of the trial, the gender of the spectators shifted from mostly male to mostly female. Reporters in the courtroom covering the trial noticed and reported on the change, but could not fully explain why. The change fueled the stories that Neal was a "ladies man."[442]

On Monday afternoon, Jim Davis, a detective working for Sheriff Boyd, was called to testify. He testified that he was incarcerated in the Douglas County jail for two weeks and was the cellmate of Ed Neal. Neal, not knowing that Davis was working undercover, told him several things, including the caliber of the gun used to kill the elderly couple. E. A. O'Brien, the editor of *The Omaha Daily Bee* newspaper, testified that he interviewed Neal in Kansas City prior to Neal knowing he was suspected in the killings. O'Brien said Neal made several contradictory statements about the murders, but also told him things that only the murderer or someone who was at the scene could have known. Shortly after the testimony of Davis and O'Brien, Mr. Mahoney rested the state's case. Mr. Estelle began Neal's defense by calling Frank Moores, who he believed could link Joe Shellenberg to the crime. Mahoney objected to the testimony in general, and Judge Clarkson ruled it inadmissible. Mr. Gurley in a surprise move rested the case for the defendant.[443]

On Wednesday morning, May 21, 1890, County Attorney Mahoney and defense attorney Lee Estelle began lengthy closing arguments. Mahoney outlined the state's case in detail. Estelle essentially clung to Neal's story of just finding unattended livestock at the farm and admitted he was guilty of rustling, but not murder. He also said that Neal's story left a doubt in the case, which was sufficient for the jury to find in favor of his client. The case went to the jury that evening. The following morning, the jury reached a verdict and pronounced Neal guilty of first degree murder. After the verdict was read, a reporter asked Neal, "what do you have to say about Shellenberg?" Neal replied, "Shellenberg killed the old Jones couple, and I disposed of the cattle and horses." Apparently Neal's assertions of Shellenberg's involvement, first at his trial, and now in the newspaper, wore thin with prosecutor Mahoney. Within a few days, Shellenberg was released from custody.[444]

The two attorneys for Neal filed a motion in the court for a new trial. On July 12, 1890, Judge Clarkson was ready to announce his decision. Neal was brought from the jail to the courthouse one more time, but this time he didn't face the jury, he stood before the judge. In a simple statement, the judge said, "in the State v. Neal the motion for a new trial will be overturned." Neal was shocked because he was certain that he would have another chance for a new trial before Judge Clarkson.[445] The judge continued by saying, "if the defendant is ready for sentencing, I will sentence him now." Mr. Estelle said that they planned on an appeal, but also said they had no grounds to challenge the sentencing. Judge Clarkson then asked Neal if he had anything to say. Neal replied, "no sir." The judge sentenced Neal to be "hung by the neck until dead," on October 25, 1890.[446]

Neal's lawyers appealed the case to the Nebraska Supreme Court. The first issue of the appeal dealt with the jury selection. The legislature had changed the law; however, the clerk was following the old process when he called potential jurors. It was the same argument that Gurley and Estelle made and lost on the opening day of the trial. During the trial, Judge Clarkson allowed the jury to visit the crime scene. In the appeal, the lawyers argued that Neal was not present during the visit and therefore was deprived of his right to be present and confront witnesses against him. Lastly, the appeal argued that evidence from one homicide should not have been admitted when trying to prove the other murder even though they happened at or near the same time. On June 29, 1891, the Supreme Court issued a lengthy ruling rejecting all of Neal's arguments. The court said, "The judgment of the district court is affirmed. The prisoner will be executed, according to law, on the 9th day of October, 1891."[447]

The first thing to be done by Sheriff Boyd was to build what the newspapers would later dub, the "death machine," or gallows. A carpenter named Julius Redowski was commissioned to construct it at a total cost of seventy-five dollars. The task was done in secrecy and once completed, stored in the basement of the courthouse after the workers had gone home.[448] The next task for Sheriff Boyd was to contract for the erection of a large sixteen foot fence at the south-west corner of the jail building to satisfy the section of the law which specified that, "such punishment (hanging) shall be inflicted in the immediate vicinity of the jail, within an enclosure to be prepared for that purpose." On the morning of October 9, 1891, the scaffold was brought from the basement of the jail. Workmen quickly assembled the gallows behind the newly constructed stockade. By the end of the day, Sheriff Boyd had everything ready for Neal to pay for his crimes.[449]

At noon on October 9, 1891, Neal stood on the scaffold and addressed the crowd. He held a crucifix in his hand as he confessed to the murders and specifically stated that he acted alone.[450] Although Neal made a full public confession of his crime and was looking into the eyes of eternity, he refused to admit his true identity.

Sheriff Boyd, who presided over the execution, took his place at the lever while Neal's arms and legs were bound. Deputy Sheriff Tierney placed the noose around the condemned man's neck, and Neal staggered as though his knees began to buckle, but "he was steadied." After placing a black "cap" over his head, Neal was moved forward onto the trap door. Sheriff Boyd wasted no time and at 12:06 P.M. pulled the lever, sending Neal downward six and one half feet.[451] News reports of the hanging differed as the *Morning World Herald* reported that Neal's neck was broken and that although there was some trembling, the body was quiet, while the *Omaha Daily Bee* reported that the neck was not broken and that death was a result of slow strangulation.[452] Both sources reported that Neal was pronounced dead at 12:37 P.M. The extensive story of Neal's execution concluded by the *World Herald's* story simply saying said that Sheriff Boyd did his duty.[453]

The secret of Neal's identity, however, was not the only mystery left unresolved by his death. No one will ever know the real nature of his relationship with Jo Clark. She was a woman who spent a great deal of time with Neal at the Douglas County Jail. Clark was a constant visitor and would later aid him in an unsuccessful attempt to escape his fate. Whether Neal was acquainted with Clark before he was incarcerated became a serious question at the time for news reporters. A friend of Clark's, Frankie Clifton, told reporters that Clark met Neal when Clark accompanied her to visit another inmate in the jail.[454] It is a fact that many of the items Neal purchased with the proceeds of his act were more than likely a present for a female companion. Was it Jo Clark? It is also a fact that Clark claimed Neal's body and made all of Neal's funeral arrangements. The Morning Edition of the *Omaha Daily Bee* made the observation that a rumor circulated in Omaha that Clark bought two cemetery lots and was planning suicide. The article continued by commenting on the rumor saying, "no one seemed to care particularly whether an additional chapter was added to the story of a man's life or not."[455] Rumors spread that grave robbers would come in the night and unearth Neal's remains. Neal was buried in an unmarked grave at Holy Sepulcher Cemetery, making the task of finding him almost impossible.[456]

One last bizarre twist in the Neal case began on July 29, 1892. Newspapers reported that Judge Joseph R. Clarkson, who was no longer a district court judge, was accidentally drowned while boating on a lake in Honey Creek, Iowa. Honey Creek is a small community approximately 20 miles northeast of Omaha.[457] The judge's body was never recovered, despite the fact that several attorneys from Omaha searched the lake for at least two weeks. After a 2 month period, the Omaha Bar Association held a memorial service for their colleague. It was said that the eulogies were so moving, "strong men were moved to tears."[458] However, on November 13, 1892, Judge Clarkson walked into his residence. His explanation was that his mind was completely blank and he had no memory of what had happened. He said he knew who he was and that he lived in Omaha, but nothing else. It was determined that he worked for an Iowa lumber company and as a farm laborer during his absence.[459]

Judge Clarkson then moved his family from Nebraska and began a law practice in Kenosha, Wisconsin. On July 14, 1909, however, the Judge disappeared again without a trace. He had a conversation with his law partner, headed for downtown Kenosha, and went missing. A frantic search turned up empty. On August 6, three weeks later, a friend of Chapman's, John Burns, who was leading a diligent search for Clarkson, found the Judge 160 miles to the east in Sabula, Iowa under the name John Paul. The judge was working in a button factory and was found sitting at machine cutting buttons from clamshells.[460] The judge was taken back to Kenosha, where he subsequently dissolved his law practice and went to work in a factory. He said he basically loved working with his hands and machines.[461] More than likely, the only machine he ever met that he didn't like was the death machine.

Sheriff John Boyd

Fuller (Joe) Shellenberg

Ed Neal

Rendering of the Penny Farm (ca. 1890)

Crowd Gathering at Neal's Hanging - October 9, 1891
Courtesy of the Douglas County Historical Society

Chapter X
Clinton E. Dixon
Death of a Soldier

Fort Niobrara in Nebraska was ostensibly established in 1879 with the expressed purpose of guarding the new Sioux Indian reservation. The Fort began operation in 1880 and was located just seven miles south of the reservation's border and forty miles from the Rosebud Agency. The implied purpose of the Fort was to protect the ranchers and settlers from any Indians who might stray from the reservation.[462] In 1882, the town of Valentine, Nebraska was established near the fort.[463] The fort operated for only a short 26 years and became obsolete when the threat of Indian attacks ended. The fort was closed in 1906 and the 16,000 acres set aside as the Niobrara National Wildlife Refuge.[464]

While in operation, both infantry and cavalry troops were garrisoned at the fort. Military officers had a different lifestyle than the enlisted men. They had special quarters and often lived with their wives at the Fort. For the enlisted men, however, life at frontier posts, including Fort Niobrara, was mostly unchanging routine and tiresome duty and drill.[465]

Because of the dull existence, purveyors of vice flocked to most all newly established army posts. Houses of ill fame, known as "hog ranches," sprung up near the forts. An example at Fort Niobrara was Casterline's Ranch, which was established just two miles from the fort. It "provided whiskey, gambling, dancing, and other entertainment for the soldiers."[466] The combination of bored soldiers and their unsavory entertainment choices became a constant problem for the respective fort commanders. Sometimes the unsavory environment caused simple altercations to intensify to the point where they turned deadly. On June 15, 1888, for example, two cavalry troopers, Sergeant Howard Nolan and Private Alexander Taylor, paid a visit to Mattie Sanderson's house of prostitution which was described as being near Fort Niobrara. The two men were in the room of a woman named Carrie Reed. The soldiers began arguing over the woman and both drew their pistols. Taylor fired first and Nolan returned fire. Nolan subsequently died, and Carrie Reed was accidentally struck and severely injured. Taylor was arrested by civil authorities.[467] Taylor was charged with murder and pled not guilty. He was tried by a jury in Cherry County and at first found guilty of manslaughter. He used a claim of self-defense, but could not convince the jury. Later, the case was re-tried and this time the jury believed him. He was found not guilty on September 27, 1888.[468]

A young "Trumpeter" named Clinton E. Dixon, of the 6th Cavalry, was not as lucky as Taylor. Dixon, originally from the area of Hanover, Pennsylvania, was posted at Fort Niobrara.[469] Dixon was 25 years old and had been a soldier for five years. Dixon was purportedly consorting with what the news media of the day dubbed as, "women of ill repute."[470] His problems began on September 29, 1891, when the Commandant became tired of the post being "seriously troubled with the presence of disorderly women," and gave orders to the Corporal of the Guard, John R. Carter, to remove any and all women found on the post.[471] A woman named Lillian Lewis, who was later identified as "Dixon's girl," was obstinate and refused the Corporal's orders to vacate the area.[472] The reports said that it was necessary for Corporal Carter to administer a "serious drubbing" to Lewis before she complied.[473] Other reports indicated that the corporal "seized a board and put to her person."[474] When Dixon, who was on furlough, heard of the mistreatment, he became very angry and vowed to get even with Carter for the treatment he imposed upon Lewis.[475]

When Dixon returned from leave the following day, September 30, 1981, he borrowed a revolver from one of his fellow soldiers.[476] Dixon went to another friend to get ammunition for the pistol, and then proceeded to the canteen to have a few drinks.[477] A short time later, he began looking for Carter and found him relaxing in his barracks, talking with several other soldiers. Dixon asked Corporal Carter to step outside and talk with him. Carter accommodated Dixon's request. As soon as the two men stepped outside and closed the door, the soldiers who stayed in the barracks heard a single pistol report.[478] The men ran to the door and found Carter clinging tightly to Dixon who was trying to flee. The mortally wounded Carter yelled at his fellow soldiers, 'Take hold of him; he has murdered me.'[479] Dixon was subdued by the soldiers and taken to the guard house, while his victim, Corporal Carter, was taken to the infirmary. Captain Carter, the troop commander, who was no relation of the victim, very meticulously took a statement from Carter as he lay dying.[480] Corporal Carter's wounds were too severe, and on October 1, 1891 he died. Corporal Carter was buried at the Fort Niobrara Post Cemetery.[481] The statement taken by Captain Carter would later become a critical part of the evidence at Dixon's trial.

Clinton E. Dixon was subsequently turned over to the custody of the United States Marshal for Nebraska, Brad Slaughter, and taken to Omaha's Douglas County jail to await legal proceedings. The Federal Government, just like today, had a contract with Douglas County, Nebraska to provide for the use of the county's jail for holding pre-trial prisoners. The United States Attorney for Nebraska, Benjamin S. Baker, took the case to the federal grand jury, and they returned an indictment of first degree murder on November 26, 1891.[482]

Dixon's trial began on December 14, 1891 in Nebraska's Circuit Court before Judge Elmer S. Dundy.[483] Dundy was the Federal Judge who presided over the trial of Standing Bear twelve years before in the Federal District Court.[484] The prosecutor was United States Attorney Benjamin S. Baker, and Clinton's defense attorney was Bernard Dolan. The crime committed by Dixon, unlike that of Taylor, was committed on the post and therefore only federal statutes applied. Because the Congress of the United States had yet to pass legislation making murder a crime, all homicides tried in the Federal Courts were tried pursuant to the United States Revised Statute §5339 which read:

"Every person who commits murder within any fort, arsenal, dockyard, magazine, or in any other place or district of country under the exclusive jurisdiction of the United States, or upon the high seas, or in any arm of the sea, or in any river, haven, creek, basin, or bay within the admiralty and maritime jurisdiction of the United States, and out of the jurisdiction of any particular state, or who, upon any such waters, maliciously strikes, stabs, wounds, poisons, or shoots at any other person, of which striking, stabbing, wounding, poisoning, or shooting such other person dies, either on land or at sea, within or without the United States, shall suffer death."[485]

The trial started with the selection of the jury, and took up the entire morning. A dozen of the perspective jurors were excused after they admitted that they would have trouble rendering a fair verdict given the fact that the death penalty was involved.[486] Baker used only six of his preemptory challenges, while Dolan used twenty-two.[487]

A number of prosecution witnesses were called, but the most damning evidence came from Captain Carter, who had taken the statement of Corporal Carter while the Corporal lay dying in the infirmary. According to the Captain, the Corporal said in an "ante-mortem" statement that Dixon called him outside of the barracks and then said to him, "Carter you planked my girl," and "you're no man." Carter said Dixon fired one shot into his abdomen.[488] According to the statement, Corporal Carter also told the Captain, "I was foully murdered by Clinton E. Dixon, and after he shot me I bit his thumb."[489]

Dixon's defense was that the actual shooting was done in self-defense. He testified that he began arguing with Carter, at which point Carter lunged at him and the two men struggled over the gun, which accidentally discharged. Dixon also testified that Corporal Carter was angry with the prostitutes involved in the post incidents as well as their regular companion soldiers, including Dixon. Dolan also was able to bring into evidence the fact that Dixon's finger did sustain a bite mark and that there were powder burns on Carter's shirt.[490]

At 10:00 A.M. on the morning of December 16, 1891, Benjamin Baker began his closing argument and summed up the government's case. Dolan began his argument, and recapped the defense's contention that the case was not premeditated murder, but simply a case of self-defense. Dolan's remarks lasted longer than Baker's, and then it was Baker's turn again at rebuttal. In his half hour summation, Baker refuted the majority of Dolan's evidence. Dixon's thumb, Baker pointed out, that was purportedly bitten by Corporal Carter, was on the same hand that Dixon used to pull out his weapon, making Dixon's story less plausible than Carter's dying declaration.[491]

Judge Dundy gave the jury a set of careful instructions, meticulously pointing out the elements of the crime and the burden of proof necessary to reach a verdict. In his instructions he began his actual charge by saying, "Now, here we are, sitting face to face, in the discharge of a difficult, important, and I might say painful duty."[492] At 4:30 in the afternoon, the jury was sent to consider the fate of Clinton E. Dixon. Within forty-five minutes, the jury was ready to render a verdict. The defendant was brought back to the courtroom and in the presence of Judge Dundy, U.S. Attorney Baker, defense attorney Dolan, and a few spectators, the jury read the verdict, "guilty as charged." Dixon lowered his head and remained standing without showing emotion.[493]

On the 18th of December, 1891, Dixon's attorney, Bernard Dolan, filed a motion for a new trial on the grounds that "the verdict was not sustained by sufficient evidence, that the verdict was contrary to law, that there were errors of law occurring at trial, and that the Court erred in giving instructions to the jury."[494] On January 7, 1892, Judge Dundy heard the oral arguments from Bernard Dolan on his motion for a new trial. Judge Dundy "called Attorney Dolan down," on the issue of faulty jury instructions.[495] On January 19, 1892, Judge Dundy answered Dolan's arguments for a new trial and denied each and every one. Also, on the 19th of January, 1892, sentence was pronounced on Dixon for his crime. The order of the Court read that Dixon was "sentenced to be committed to the custody of the United States Marshal for the District of Nebraska, to be confined to the county jail of Douglas County, Nebraska, in said State, until the 22nd day of April 1892, at which time between the hours of ten o'clock A.M. and four o'clock P.M. of said day and in said County and State, and by the said Marshal, to be hanged by the neck until dead."[496]

Dixon's only appeal from the Judge's decision, based upon the fact that it was made in the United States Circuit Court, was to the United States Supreme Court. In 1892, in order to appeal a case to the Supreme Court, the defendant was required to pay for the transcripts of the case. Although Mr. Dolan as well as Mr. Baker tried to obtain a waiver to allow Dixon to use "back pay" to pay for the transcripts, the plea went unanswered and the time limit for the appeal lapsed.[497] The last alternative for Dolan to save Clinton Dixon was to ask President Benjamin Harrison to commute Dixon's sentence to life imprisonment. Dolan did exactly that.[498] Dolan's appeal contained a personal plea from Dixon who confessed to the crime and added two mitigating factors. He said he was intoxicated and that the crime was committed during a sudden impulse. Dolan's plea was joined by five of the original jurors and as well as Judge Dundy.[499] On April 6, 1892, President Harrison sent back his answer saying that he reviewed the facts of the case, and "under those circumstances I cannot interfere."[500]

It was then apparent that the hanging of Dixon must take place, but the idea of another execution at the jail did not sit well with the Douglas County Commissioners. It was only a little over six months since the execution of Ed Neal, which turned out to be a precursor to the storming of the jail and the lynching of a man named Joe Coe. Not only was Coe lynched, but the mob caused serious destruction of the jail. Two of the Commissioners, "Berlin and Paddock," told Marshal Slaughter that if he wanted to 'kill his man,' it could be better done at Fort Omaha, after all, they said, he was a soldier.[501] Marshal Slaughter's contention was that Douglas County's contract with the Federal Government included carrying out the provisions of the "full extent of the law," and extended to the use of jail grounds as a place of execution.[502] The County Commissioners went on record by passing a resolution to the effect that they were opposed to the fact that Dixon would be executed on county property. In addition, Commissioner Paddock offered a second resolution pointing out the fact that the date set for Dixon's hanging happened to be Arbor Day, a holiday observed by Douglas County's Government.[503] Marshal Slaughter notified President Harrison, who issued a "respite" for Dixon until May 20, 1892.[504] The President's telegram read in part, "I have respited the execution of the sentence in the case of C. E. Dixon, until Friday May 20, 1892, and you will act accordingly." Marshal Slaughter knew that "act accordingly," meant that he would have to carry out the execution of Dixon.

Omaha's Coliseum Exhibition was an annual fall event that included a variety of things for the public to do as well see. The 1891 event included music, booths, vendors, and curiosities, including the "gallows upon which the murderer Ed Neal paid the penalty for his devilish crime." After the Exposition, the gallows was given to the Coliseum Commission, dismantled, and placed in storage.[505]

Marshal Slaughter contacted the Coliseum Commission, and made arrangements to rent the gallows. He paid workers to dismantle it and re-erect it in Douglas County's jail yard. He also paid to have the apparatus re-fitted with an electrical device that was capable of releasing the trap doors. In addition, three buttons would replace the one lever used to send Neal to eternity. Only one button would be wired to the electric latch, and be the actual switch that opened the trap.[506] The purpose of using two blind and one live switch would be similar to the common practice of firing squads. One rifle was always loaded with blanks. In the latter example, theoretically each member of the firing squad may be able to rationalize that they did not fire a fatal shot. It seemed as though the Marshal was ready to "act accordingly," but circumstances dictated that he would ask President Harrison for another delay.

Marshal Slaughter also wore the hat of Grand Master of the Nebraska Free Masons, and it just so happened that a major conclave of the Nebraska Masons was being held in Omaha on

May 20, 1892, and it fell upon the Marshal to preside over the events of that particular day. Marshal Slaughter sent the President a telegram and asked for an additional week for Dixon.[507] The President issued a new "respite," and set the new date of the hanging for June 24, 1892.[508]

On June 21, 1892, Bernard Dolan publicly announced that the President should commute Dixon's sentence because it was the "expressed wish of the people of Douglas County," but even as Dolan grasped at straws to find a way to save his client, the marshal was testing "Ed Neal's death machine." [509]

Several days before Dixon was scheduled to be hung, Marshal Slaughter told all who asked that he planned on conducting the execution somewhere between 3 and 4 O'clock in the afternoon. That was not the marshal's plan. It was a clever ruse used in hopes that a rumor of the later time would spread, and keep the curious throng away from the jail. *The Omaha Daily Bee* reported that the marshal wanted to delay the execution until the last possible moment.[510]

In reality, Slaughter and his deputies arrived at the jail in the morning with the death warrant in hand. The marshal stood in front of Dixon's cell at 10:40 AM and read the warrant. Slaughter asked Dixon if he had anything to say at that point, and Dixon told him no. The group of men, including Father Rigge, a Catholic priest, quickly marched to the west door of the jail and into the makeshift courtyard surrounded by a stockade fence.[511] The men ascended the steps of the gallows and Father Rigge knelt in prayer while the deputy marshals placed the noose around Dixon's neck and strapped his ankles, knees, and wrists. As the deputies adjusted the cap on Dixon's head, his silent prayers were noticeable because of his moving lips. At 11:02 A.M., Marshal Slaughter, Deputy Hastings, and Deputy Harris stood at equal distance and at the count of 'one, two, three,' each simultaneously pushed the buttons that released the trap, and Dixon fell through the opening.[512] The "drop" produced only a "few muscular contractions in the legs," and the body became "motionless."[513] It was estimated that "from the time the condemned man ascended the scaffold until the trap was sprung was just thirty seconds."[514] The attending physicians pronounced Dixon dead at 11:13 A.M., and his body was removed from beneath the gallows at 11:29.[515] Shortly after the hanging, Father Rigge arranged for a Catholic funeral to be held at St. Philomena's Church, with the burial to be at Holy Sepulcher Cemetery, which, coincidentally, is the resting place of Ed Neal.[516]

In another ironic twist, Lillian Lewis, the woman who was "planked" by Corporal Carter, was being held in the Douglas County Jail. She was in Omaha and became involved in an altercation. She received a term in jail for fighting which happened to be on the same day as the scheduled execution. She was fearful that after the hanging, a mob may storm the jail and lynch her due to the fact that she caused the death of both Carter and Dixon. She asked for protection, but was told that the only true place she could be safe was in the cell to be vacated by Dixon. Jailers told her that it was also the same cell that held Ed Neal and kept him safe for several months. She was superstitious and not too keen on the idea; however, her fear of the mob overrode her angst, and she decided to spend the night in the cell.[517] She told the jailers the next morning that she had several visitors in the night, not the lynch mob she feared, but the ghosts of Ed Neal and Clinton Dixon. Lewis told the guards she had extensive conversations with both Neal and Corporal Dixon.[518]

Fort Niobrara (ca. 1886)
Original Courtesy Nebraska State Historical Society

Judge Elmer S. Dundy
Courtesy Douglas County Historical Society

**United States Marshal
Brad Slaughter**
Courtesy Masonic Grand Lodge
Of Nebraska

Benjamin S. Baker

Chapter XI
Harry Hill
Bad Cop

The town of Weeping Water is located in Cass County, in the southeastern part of Nebraska. There are at least three renditions of how the town was named. The fact is, however, that the name simply evolved by mistaken translation. The early Indians, either Pawnee or Otoe, named the area "Nigahoe" which meant rustling water. When white men arrived, they began pronouncing the name "Nigahoage," which was actually another Indian word meaning water that weeps, hence weeping water.[519]

In the 1880s, the area was a thriving agricultural part of the state, with a healthy mixture of immigrant farmers who helped establish strong work, religious, and community ethics responsible for making the area prosper. Matthew (Mattes) Akeson was one of those farmers, and considered a pillar of the community. He was born in Sweden and immigrated to America in 1854 at the age of 29. In 1862, during the Civil War, he felt a duty to his new country and enlisted in the army, and was assigned to Company H, 102 Illinois Infantry. He served with General Sherman, and under the command of the general, made the infamous march to the sea. After he was discharged, he made his way west to Mills County in Iowa where he met and married Rebecca Gentry, a widow with 3 children. They married and moved to Nebraska; where they settled and began farming 480 acres 2 miles northeast of Weeping Water in Cass County. The couple had three children of their own.[520] In the 1889 book, The Portrait and Biographical Album of Otoe and Cass Counties, Nebraska, Akeson was described as, "noted for his uprightness and manly qualities and in all matters of business his word is considered as good as his bond."[521]

In the late fall of 1893, it was harvest time for Nebraska's farmers, and the Akeson farm was bustling. The elderly Akeson, then 68 years old, relied heavily on his son, Tom, and Gus Burke, their regular hired hand, to work the farm. The fall of 1883 produced a bumper crop, and there was so much corn to be husked that the Akesons hired extra help to get it from the fields. On Monday, October 30, 1893, Tom Akeson was in Swindle's saloon in Weeping Water, and by chance, happened to meet two men. They both had the appearance of having worked outdoors, and since the farm needed help, Tom struck up a conversation. He asked the men if they knew how to husk corn, and the taller of the two said that he just finished a job for a farmer who lived near Omaha. Tom hired the two men on the spot, and the three men headed for the Akeson farm.[522]

The taller man told Tom his name was George Rogers and the second introduced himself as John Benwell. When they arrived at the farm, they were given supper and a place to sleep for the night. They were up bright and early the next morning and spent the entire day in the field harvesting corn. On Wednesday, November 1, they got up and ate their breakfast. As soon as they finished, the elder Akeson told the pair that he needed to use the wagon to haul hogs to market in Louisville, Nebraska, and there would be no harvesting that day. He paid them for Tuesday's work, thanked them, and let them go.[523] The two disappointed men took their wages and headed back to Weeping Water and Swindle's saloon. They drank and played billiards until after lunch. Sometime in the afternoon, they decided to go to Louisville. Along the way, the two talked about going back to the Akeson farm, and relieving Matthew of the proceeds from his hog sale. They hadn't quite made up their minds, but went back to Weeping Water where Benwell bought a pistol at the hardware store.[524]

Matthew and Rebecca Akeson had supper with their son Tom and hired man Chris Burke that Wednesday evening. Peter Simeon, a man hired just that day to replace Rogers and Benwell, also took supper with them that evening. After dinner Tom and Matthew retired to the den to have a cigar. Suddenly, without warning, the door burst open and the two masked bandits rushed into the house yelling and screaming for Matt to raise his hands. The elderly gentleman was apparently confused at the situation and did not immediately comply. For his unhurried response, Rogers rewarded him with a bullet to the chest. Gus Burke jumped up and rushed towards the shooter. For his bravery, he was shot in the head, but the bullet struck him at an odd angle and ricocheted off his head, luckily leaving him with just a deep scalp wound. Almost simultaneously with Burke's lunge, Tom Akeson tried to subdue the gunman and they struggled. Tom was repelled with a gunshot wound thorough his wrist, but he managed to get a look at the gunman's face when he lost his mask in the scuffle. Peter Simeon, the new man, also jumped up during the fracas and was shot through the knee. Meanwhile, the second bandit was busy beating Rebecca with what at the time was believed to be a wooden club. At that point both men panicked and fled the scene empty handed, leaving Matthew Akeson dead and everyone else injured.[525]

Burke, bleeding profusely from the head, was able to reach a neighbor's farm. He told the neighbor what happened, and they quickly triggered a search for the two outlaws. Descriptions of the killers and the account of the botched robbery were hastily printed in the local newspapers. On Thursday, the dragnet snagged several persons in the small Cass County towns of Union, South Bend, and Weeping Water, but they were released because they didn't fit the descriptions. Two tramps were taken into custody at Fairbury, Nebraska at the railroad depot. The men purportedly matched the description, but were more than likely arrested merely because there were two of them. They were held for additional identification, but later released.[526]

On Friday evening, two days after the murder, 30 miles west of Weeping Water in Lincoln, Nebraska, John Conway was sitting in a saloon at 20th and "O" Street reading an account of the incident. After Conway finished reading the article, he couldn't help but notice that the two strangers in the saloon matched the description of the suspects. He surreptitiously sent word to the police station, and within minutes both men were in custody.[527]

Chief of Police Cooper and Detective Malone questioned and then searched the men. One man who identified himself as Rogers had identifying papers with the name Harry Hill in his wallet. He told the officers his real name was Harry Hill and that he was 27 years old. Hill also had on his person a loaded .38 caliber Bulldog revolver. The second man gave his name as John Benwell and he told the officers that he was 21. Hill and Benwell were taken to the Lincoln city jail and held on a charge of vagrancy. Chief Cooper then contacted Cass County Sheriff William Tighe at Plattsmouth, Nebraska, which is the county seat of Cass County. His wire told of the apprehension, and he added in his wire that the men matched the description and were more than likely the two wanted men. The sheriff wired back that he would be there in the morning with Tom Akeson who would be able to positively identify the wanted men.[528]

The next morning, the sheriff sent his brother Deputy John Tighe and Deputy Ed Fitzgerald to Lincoln with Tom Akeson. When Akeson saw Hill and Benwell at the Lincoln city jail, there was no hesitation in his identification. He said it was Hill who shot and killed his father and wounded the others. Based upon the identification, Cass County Attorney Harvey Travis went to M. Archer, justice of the peace, and obtained warrants for the two men on charges of first degree murder. Sheriff Tighe advised his deputies to arrest the men and bring them by train to Plattsmouth. He said the warrants would be waiting upon their arrival.[529]

The train from Lincoln was due in Plattsmouth at 11:00 A.M. Saturday morning, and by 10:00, A.M. nearly 1,000 Cass County farmers were gathered at the station to welcome the two suspects. Sheriff Tighe knew that the part of the welcome festivities would include a couple of ropes and a telegraph pole. He deputized an additional 20 men to help get the prisoners from the train to the jail. The train was on time, and as it slowly pulled into the station, the baggage door slid open and the conductor yelled to the crowd that the prisoners were not on board. The mob was worked up and didn't believe conductor. A committee was allowed to search the train to verify that they were not hidden somewhere on the train. The committee yelled at the mob that the conductor was being truthful, and the deputies and their prisoners would probably be on the next train.[530]

Meanwhile the crowd was growing and had doubled in size. It was becoming apparent, that even with 20 extra deputies, Sheriff Tighe couldn't prevent a lynching, and more than likely there would be serious bloodshed. County Attorney Travis knew that the deputies were on the next train, and quickly sent a wire to them unbeknownst to the sheriff. The wire intercepted the train at Ashland, Nebraska and it directed deputies Tighe and Fitzgerald to take their prisoners to the Douglas County jail in Omaha and board them there. When the noon train arrived at Plattsmouth without the entourage, the crowd blamed the sheriff. He was able to legitimately say he had no idea what happened to his deputies and their prisoners. Later, when Travis told him that the men were diverted to Omaha, the sheriff knew he dodged a bullet. He thankfully watched as the crowd slowly dissipated.[531]

As soon as the two suspects were booked into the Douglas County jail, they were separated and one of the jailers began asking questions. The jailer, Theodore Bennett, told Benwell that he should make a voluntary statement. Benwell complied and began a narrative of the events surrounding the murder, while Bennett took detailed notes during his confession. When he completed his story, Bennett asked if it was the truth. Benwell was asked if he would sign the confession and he signed it "John Benwell." The Cass County deputies, John Tighe and Ed Fitzgerald, signed after Benwell as witnesses.[532]

Although County Attorney Travis filed first degree murder complaints against Harry Hill and John Benwell on November 16, 1893, they were held at the Douglas County jail until their arraignment on December 11th. During that time, several things changed in Cass County. The 1893 election brought a new sheriff to Cass County. That December, the community's anger towards the two suspected killers, at least on the surface, did not seem as intense. However, the new sheriff, J.C. Eikenbary, who had not as yet been sworn in, and outgoing Sheriff Tighe were worried that there may be some who were capable of sparking another mob scene. They decided to be prudent and add more staff. On the morning of the arraignment, deputies John Tighe and Ed Fitzgerald brought Hill and Benwell by train to Plattsmouth.[533]

The two men were brought before District Court Judge Sam Chapman. Chapman presided over the trials of train wreckers Hoffman and Bell in Otoe County 6 years earlier, and was a highly competent judge. The state was represented by Cass County Attorney Harvey D. Travis. Matthew Gering, a prominent Cass County attorney, represented both Hill and Benwell. The majority of the day was occupied with legal wrangling between opposing attorneys. Gering began by asking the arraignment be postponed for 24 hours. Judge Chapman eventually satisfied the concerns of everyone, and both men pled not guilty to all charges. The judge decided that since selecting an impartial jury would be difficult, the process would begin the following day. Reporters asked Travis if he had concerns about the people taking matters into their own hands. He responded by saying the defendants should be safe, but added the caveat, "as long as the jury doesn't render a verdict of not guilty."[534]

Tuesday's trial began with Gering's concerns over the legal sufficiency of the original indictments. Judge Chapman eventually ruled against Gering's defendants. Gering then asked the judge to separate the cases. Chapman agreed and stipulated that the case of Harry Hill would be heard first, followed by Benwell's. The remainder of the day was occupied with jury selection.[535]

On Wednesday, December 13, 1893, the morning session of the trial continued with seating a jury. In the afternoon, the jury heard opening arguments and the court began taking testimony from the state's witnesses. The state introduced medical evidence detailing the fatal wounds. Next, several witnesses placed Hill and

Benwell near the farmstead. The most damaging testimony came on the following morning. Rebecca Akeson told the story of her husband's murder in graphic detail, and her son, Tom, made an eyewitness identification of Hill. County Attorney Travis called several more witnesses, including the coroner who produced the fatal bullet taken from the body of Matt Akeson. The prosecutor had an additional 22 witnesses scheduled to testify, but decided they would not be necessary. He rested the state's case.[536]

Harry Hill's defense was based upon his own testimony. He began by confirming many people involved in the case suspected. "My real name is Ed L Smith, he said." He also confirmed that he was about 30 years old and was once a Washington, D. C. policeman. He said he was fired for conduct unbecoming an officer. Hill then methodically traced his problems with drinking to when he was a child in South Carolina. He began drinking at 8 years of age and said, "I drank liquor every day." He detailed his military service and with each part of the story he included the fact that problems with alcohol led to all of his other problems. He said that he re-enlisted and was charged criminally after being drunk and involved in a stabbing incident. He was sent to Leavenworth prison for a short time, and then dishonorably discharged. He testified that on the day of the murder, he and Benwell went to Weeping Water and while they played pool, he drank about 16 or 17 whiskeys.[537]

After Hill's testimony, Mr. Gering continued with the introduction of an affidavit from Hill's senior officer verifying the fact that Hill was a habitual drunkard during the time he spent in the military. The defense continued with several Cass County physicians testifying about the effects of alcohol and the problems associated with its excessive use. With little else available, Gering rested his case. The rest of the afternoon was spent with the prosecution examining rebuttal witnesses.[538]

On Saturday, December 16, court convened at 9:00 A.M., and Judge Chapman began with an extensive list of instructions for the jury. The process consumed the morning and final arguments began after lunch. Mr. Gering's argument was based upon the habitual effects of Hill's protracted drinking. The prosecution's closing took much longer with Mr. Travis going over each step of the crime and telling how the evidence supported the state's case. The jury retired at 4:15 to determine Hill's fate. The jury deliberated though Saturday. On Sunday, after 22 hours of deliberation, the jury finally reached a verdict. They found Ed L.

Smith, alias Harry Hill, guilty of murder in the first degree and set his punishment as death by hanging.[539]

On Monday morning, December 18, 1893, the day following Hill's conviction, the trial of John Benwell began. It was the same cast of characters that participated in the Hill trial. Veteran Judge Samuel Chapman was in-charge; County Attorney Travis led the prosecution for the state, and Matthew Gering tried to mount a reasonable defense for Benwell. Before proceedings got underway, it was Mr. Gering's turn to confirm a suspicion. He began by telling the court that his client's actual name was John Benwell Kruse. By 10:00 A.M. the following morning, a jury had been seated. The county attorney's opening remarks were strong and indicated that John B. Kruse would be prosecuted with the same vigor as was his companion. Mr. Gering waived his opening argument. Speculation around the buzzing courthouse was that the defense would try and mitigate Benwell's involvement by placing most of the blame on Hill.[540]

The state's case began with the testimony of several witnesses, including the hired hand Simeon and Rebecca Akeson, who said they believed that Benwell also had a pistol and was firing during the melee. When Tom Akeson was called to the stand, he essentially gave the same testimony as he did at the Hill trial. Dr. W. H. Dearing, who also happened to be the clerk of the district court, was at the Akeson residence shortly after the shooting, and described Matthew's body and wounds. John Unruh, Cass County Coroner, testified concerning how he acquired possession of the bullet introduced in the Hill case. The major evidence in the case against Benwell came in the form of the confession he made at the Douglas County jail. The state established the foundation for the confession with the testimony of Theodore Bennett, the jailer who interrogated Benwell and obtained the confession. Mr. Travis also took the testimony of deputies Tighe and Fitzpatrick, who witnessed Benwell's confession. Gering cross examined the witnesses in a futile attempt to keep the confession out of evidence. Judge Chapman allowed the damaging statements of Benwell into the record.[541]

Harry Hill was brought to the stand to testify. His testimony corroborated in almost every detail the confession made by Benwell at the Douglas County jail. Hill said that he was the only one with a pistol, and it was the one that Benwell bought at Weeping Water and the same one taken from him by the Lincoln police at the time of his arrest. Then John Benwell Kruse took the stand and began by surprising many in the courtroom when he admitted that he too was once a law enforcement officer. Benwell said he was born in Ottawa, Canada, and went to a Jesuit school until he was 16 years old. At age 17 he joined the Northwestern Police. After a few years on the force, he left and traveled the northwest part of the United States, working on farms and doing other odd jobs. He ended up in Omaha and then worked his way to Cass County. He then repeated the same story, which had been corroborated by Hill.[542]

The defense called Drs. Shipman and Livingston, who both testified that Benwell had a "weak mind." In essence, Gering was trying to prove that the younger Benwell was highly influenced by the elder Hill, and that he should not be held as accountable as Hill. In rebuttal, Travis called several witnesses, including Dr. W. H. Schildknecht and William Clements, who testified that Tom Akeson had originally told them that Benwell had fired the fatal shot. The prosecutor called A. W. and John Magney, who testified that Benwell worked for them at Union, Nebraska and seemed perfectly normal.[543]

On Thursday afternoon, December 21, 1893, after four days of trial, both attorneys made their closing arguments, and Judge Chapman charged the jury. They deliberated all day Friday, and on Saturday at 3:20 P. M., after being out nearly 48 hours, the jury rendered its verdict. They found him guilty of murder in the first degree and recommended a sentence of life imprisonment. As soon as the verdict was read, Judge Chapman passed sentence on Benwell and added a caveat. He said that if the discretion was up to him, Benwell would hang with Hill. Exactly 38 minutes later, Sheriff Tighe, with paperwork in hand, was on the train to the Nebraska Penitentiary in Lincoln with an iron laden John Benwell Kruse. There were many in Cass County that felt the same about Benwell's punishment as did Judge Chapman, and even more who were sure that his expeditious departure saved his life.[544] News accounts simply said, "the general public in Cass County was highly dissatisfied with the verdict in the case."[545] He would spend Christmas Eve in prison, and was lucky to be alive.

The judge took off Christmas Day, but was back in court on December 26th. It was time for Harry Hill's Christmas present. It wasn't a new trial, like the one requested by his attorney, Mr. Gering, as a matter of fact, the judge ruled against it. It was Hill's sentence. The judge began with a polite command by saying, "Harry Hill, you may stand up." He then asked Harry if he had anything to say, to which Hill simply replied, "nothing." After saying, "nothing," however, Hill told the judge that he felt that he didn't get a fair trial and said that if the trial would have been held outside of Cass County, then maybe he could have gotten a fair trial. Judge Chapman synopsized the case and outlined in detail why Hill's trial was fair and impartial. The judge then set the date for Hill's hanging as April 13, 1894, "between the hours of 10:00 O'clock in the forenoon and 3:00 O'clock in the afternoon of said day." He added that the sheriff was to hang him by the neck until he was dead. Hill seemed to accept his fate, but was still angry about the outcome of Benwell's trial. He felt, as did most of the people of Cass County, that he should have company on the scaffold.[546]

There was a small minority of citizens, however, that didn't share the opinion that Hill should hang. Just as the ladies uncharacteristically flocked to Ed Neal, there was a similar attraction to Harry Hill. Women associated with church groups brought food and flowers to the condemned man. One news article described his cell as, "a flower garden on a small scale."[547] A story in the *Evening World Herald* said that, "He has quite a number of lady visitors of all degrees and classes," and went on to ascribe him as somewhat of a celebrity. Speaking of the women visitors, the story said, "they nearly always request him to give them his autograph, or something similar, to remember him by, and he always accommodates them." The newspaper also said that the subject of Hill's conversations mostly concern his newly found Catholic religion or the evils of drinking, but more often the latter. Hill was quoted in the article as saying saloons, "are the kindergartens of the criminal."[548] Harlan Seyfer, Plattsmouth Historian, in his article, *The Ladies and the Murderer*, explains the attraction by linking it to Plattsmouth's chapter of the Women's Christian Temperance Union.[549] The WCTU was becoming a significant social force at the end of 19th Century with a national membership of 158,477 in 1891.[550] Mr. Seyfer's conjecture concerning the attraction to Hill, at least in part, may also explain why Ed Neal had such a strong female following.

On March 20, 1894, a little over 3 weeks before the hanging, the Nebraska Supreme Court agreed to hear an appeal filed by Attorney Gering on behalf of Ed. L. Smith (aka Harry Hill). Their acceptance of the case triggered an automatic stay of execution.[551] Gering's appeal contained 15 points of contention, beginning with an attack on the sufficiency of the original filing of the charges and ending with the inadequacy of the evidence to support the death penalty. The justices answered each of the arguments one-by-one, and disallowed each argument point by point. On

November 8, 1894, they issued their ruling and affirmed the actions of the district court.[552] In January, 1895, the court set the new date for Harry Hill's hanging as Friday, March 1, 1895.[553]

By the first part of February, 1895, Sheriff Eikenbary's plans for the Hanging of Harry Hill were nearly complete. His carpenters were on call ready to build the required privacy enclosure and gallows next to the jail. He planned on waiting until the week before the scheduled execution before completing the work in the event that Governor Holcomb might grant Hill clemency and reduce his sentence.[554] On February 23, there was late word from the Governor that he would not interfere with the hanging. The sheriff's carpenters began their work on the north side of the jail building. All of the noise created by the construction was within earshot of Hill.[555]

Hill was not affected by the preparations for his death. He had immersed himself so deeply in his religion that he became almost indifferent to the fact that he would soon be dead. The evening before the hanging, his spiritual advisor, Father Carney, left after being with him all day. Hill had a strong dislike for the press, but granted a final interview after supper. Sheriff Eikenbary began by telling reporters that he never had a better behaved prisoner than Hill. Hill's comment to one question was that he was content and that the truth had set him free. He told the press that he was confident because he was assured of his salvation. Hill was asked if he thought there were some people that would be satisfied to see him pay for his crime on the gallows. The contented Hill abruptly ended the interview.[556]

Sheriff Eikenbary had approximately 200 special passes printed to the execution, which would purportedly allow access to the enclosure. Because of the nature of the crime, the near lynching of Hill and Benwell, and because it would be Cass County's first execution, Sheriff Eikenbary predicted a massive crowd. The sheriff spread the word that the hanging would occur around 1 P.M., but told those holding tickets to be sure and be there by 9:00 A.M. When the deputies opened the access doors, only about 100 of the 200 ticket holders were waiting to be admitted to the enclosure.[557]

Shortly after 9:00 A.M., ex-sheriff Tighe entered from the jail and took his place on the scaffold. Sheriff Eikenbary and several of his deputies were next to climb to the top of the platform. Smith (aka Hill), was led from the building by Fathers Nugent and Cook. Father Carney, who had spent most of the time counseling Hill, became ill and had to leave. Hill stood on the trap door while the priests prayed and gave him final absolution. When they were finished, they stepped away and Deputy Holloway secured his hands and bound his legs together. He previously asked sheriff Eikenbary not to ask him for any last words, so when he was secured, the sheriff placed the black hood over his head followed by the noose. At 9:08, A.M., before the crowd realized what was happening, Sheriff Eikenbary pulled the lever, which sent Hill through the trap door. His body bounced slightly from the give in the rope, and then his neck was broken and he lost consciousness. A total of 9 physicians quickly attended Hill, including Dr. Livingston, who had testified at the trial. Hill was pronounced dead 14 minutes after the fall. Hill's body was cut down after a few minutes and the door to the enclosure was opened. His body was left on display long enough for the curious to walk past and look.[558] A Catholic funeral was held the following morning. Services were conducted by Father Carney, and Hill was buried in the Catholic cemetery. Ed. L. Smith (aka Harry Hill) was 31.[559]

John Benwell Kruse, Hill's partner in the murder, was serving his life sentence in Nebraska's penitentiary in Lincoln on the day Hill was hanged. Unfortunately, John Benwell Kruse had become ill from consumption (tuberculosis) during his incarceration. The physicians who were caring for Benwell were convinced that he was dying. In the summer of 1899, Governor Poynter issued a full pardon to Kruse based upon his terminal illness.[560] When the news reached the people of Cass County, they became irate. Subsequent stories railed the fact that persons who had actually seen Benwell at the penitentiary said he did not appear ill in the least. In October, 1900, stories appeared in the newspapers which criticized the fact that procedures were not followed by the Governor prior to the pardon and called it a "secret deal."[561] The people of Cass County who are aware of the case will say that once Benwell Kruse walked out of the door, he headed back to Canada and was never heard of again. They say he got away with murder.[562]

Harvey D. Travis

Mattthew Gering

Harry Hill

Cass County Court House (ca. 1893)

Chapter XII
Claude Hoover
Swift Justice

Eighteenth Century Italian criminologist Cesare Beccaria in his <u>Essay on Crimes and Punishments</u> addressed the issue of punishment. In the part of his work titled, *Of the Advantage of immediate Punishment*, he said, "The more immediately after the commission of a crime, a punishment is inflicted, the more just and useful it will be."[563] British statesman William Gladstone is most often credited with being the first to use the phrase, "justice delayed is justice denied." Even our forefathers were concerned that trials should be speedy when they crafted the sixth amendment. What is a speedy trial? In Nebraska's Douglas County District Court, the record time for a case moving through the court was set in 1895. It took only 16 days from the arrest of the suspect until the conviction of the defendant by a jury. A story in *The Omaha Daily Bee* noted the fact that, "the trial furnished a record breaker for the county."[564] In reality, the case may have moved even faster had the court not taken time off at Christmas. In 1895, there were many who thought the case may have stretched the idea of swift justice a little too far; thereby making it unjust. The defendant in the record breaking case was Claude H. Hoover.

Claude Hoover was born in Hamilton, Missouri in 1863. In 1890, the twenty-seven year old Hoover moved to Omaha and lived with his mother and step-father whose last names were Brophy. They lived in a residence at 1811 South Eleventh Street. Claude had a step-sister, Katie Brophy, and another sister who was married to an Omaha police officer named Sam DuBois.[565] By December of 1895, the industrious DuBois had moved on from the police department, and was managing a coal company as well as an elevator repair service. The shop was located on 13th and Howard Streets. To help get his fledgling business running, DuBois employed his brother-in-law, Claude Hoover, to assist him by repairing elevators. He also used his sister-in-law, seventeen year old Katie Brophy, to run the office. Besides being a cop,

DuBois was also involved in Omaha's politics and had been a political figure around town for several years. In 1895, he was a recently elected member of Omaha's City Council.[566] He was a large, gregarious man who had a great sense of humor. His size and personality made him a good cop, but even better politician. One political anecdote in particular typified both his bearing. An opponent tried to get under his skin by saying, "Some of Sam DuBois friends made him a present of a cake of soap the other day."[567] DuBois responded by saying that he was incensed of the insinuation by his political rival that he didn't use soap. The report quoted his response as, "he said that he takes a bath every year, on the first day of May, whether he needs it or not."[568] There was one person, unfortunately, who could annoy DuBois, and that was his brother-in-law.

On December 13, 1895, Claude went into the office and scolded his stepsister, Katie. She was socializing with another girl in the office, and Hoover didn't approve of her.[569] Mrs. DuBois, Hoover's sister, later said she believed the scolding was based upon the fact that Katie was seeing a boy named Babe Nicklis, who Hoover didn't like.[570] Katie was very sensitive and didn't take criticism well. She began crying even before Hoover was finished with his lecture. It was about 1:30 P.M., and by chance, DuBois happened into the office and saw what was happening between Hoover and his stepsister. DuBois said to Hoover, in a protective tone, "I don't want you fussing over that girl," to which Hoover replied, "that's none of your business."[571] DuBois became uncharacteristically angry and grabbed his brother-in-law by the arm, shoving him towards the door.[572] DuBois said, "get out of here; you damned miserable whelp and coward."[573] As DuBois pushed Hoover out the door, he told Sam he had wages coming and he wanted to be paid. DuBois told Hoover that didn't have a lot of cash on him or in the office, but he would borrow a few dollars and pay him what he was owed. DuBois decided to go to a neighboring business where he knew he could borrow some money to pay Hoover. His friend lent him two dollars, and with what he already had, he was able to pay Hoover twelve dollars and fifty cents. Meanwhile, as DuBois was running the errand, Katie made her stepbrother promise that there would be no further trouble between the two men. Hoover apparently raised his right hand and said that he would swear that there would be no more trouble as far as he was concerned. When DuBois returned, Hoover said, "I'm very much obliged to you," and DuBois said, "your welcome."[574] One of the first things that Hoover did after leaving DuBois was go to a pawn shop, owned by Abraham Singer which was located on Douglas street, and buy a .38 caliber American Bulldog revolver for $1.90.[575]

Witnesses would later place Hoover in several saloons after he left the pawnshop. He spent the afternoon drinking and spending most of the money he was paid by DuBois. About 3:00 P.M., Brophy got a telephone message from her step brother, Claude, who said he wanted to meet her on Howard Street across from the office. A few minutes later, he appeared at the meeting location and waved to Brophy signaling her to cross the street and talk to him. For some reason, even though DuBois was not there, he didn't want to go back to the office. Brophy said that Hoover, at the time of the meeting, seemed to be intoxicated. Hoover told her he was leaving town and headed to Kansas City.[576] In the same breath, he made the comment, "Sam had no business to stick his nose into that, and he should be sorry that he did." He continued by telling her, "I would have done right if I had shot him." Hoover then promised Brophy again that he would not cause any problems with DuBois.[577]

Hoover was well known and frequented several businesses near the office. He had a habit of just stopping by and chatting with business people while they worked. He was well liked and accepted by most in the neighborhood. One of his frequent hangouts was a shoe store located at 418 ½ South 13th Street, owned by Gustave Saafeldt. According to Saafeldt, sometime between 1:00 and 2:00 P.M., Hoover came into his store and told him that he had been fired from his job. The shopkeeper said that he didn't stick around to talk; he just turned around and left. Hoover came back to the store around 5:30 that evening. According to Gustave, his brother Charlie Saafeldt and a man named Andrew Jackson were also in the store when Hoover came in the second time. Hoover sat down on a bench and said, "I would give a quarter if Sam DuBois would show up."[578]

About fifteen minutes later, Hoover got his wish as DuBois walked into the store and said, "Good evening gentlemen." Hoover stood up and said, "I've got you where I want you, you *expletive deleted*." Hoover then fired two shots at DuBois at almost point blank range. With both hands, DuBois grabbed Hoover's wrist and the gun and said, "you coward why did you shoot me?"[579] DuBois then wrested the gun away from Hoover and dragged him outside onto the sidewalk. DuBois was much bigger and stronger than Hoover, and he wrestled Hoover into the drugstore, which happened to be right next to the shoe store. DuBois asked the druggist, Broadwell Bell, if he would call the doctor, and said Hoover just shot him. The drunken Hoover, who was still being held by DuBois, said, "Yes, I shot you. I told you I would the first time I saw you." DuBois by this time had control of the gun and handed it to a bystander, James Fenton. DuBois told Fenton, "Take the gun. He shot me, but I don't want to shoot him."[580] DuBois then took off his coat and stretched it across the counter. The druggist helped DuBois into the back room and insisted that he lay on the couch. Dr. J. E. Summers was the first to arrive. He ordered that DuBois be taken to Presbyterian Hospital, which was located nearby at 13th and Dodge, just a few blocks from the shoe store.[581] The police arrived shortly after the incident and arrested Hoover.

When DuBois was admitted to the hospital, it was determined that his only hope was to undergo surgery to remove the two bullets still inside his thick torso. Drs. Summers, Allison, and Coulter began the operation at 8:30 P.M. The team quickly determined that both bullets did a significant amount of damage. After operating for an hour, they were able to extract one of the slugs, but couldn't locate the second bullet. Mrs. DuBois, along with her two young daughters, waited patiently to hear from the doctors. The surgeons told Mrs. DuBois that the outlook for her husband was not good due to a significant amount of internal damage.[582] Ex-policeman and City Councilman Sam DuBois died of his injuries on December 14, 1895 shortly after 3:00 P.M.

DuBois' funeral was held two days later on December 16, 1895 at 2:00 P.M. The funeral was conducted from the family's residence at 13th and Valley Streets, and the procession went from the home to Laurel Hill Cemetery near 21st and Polk Streets, where he was interred. Sam DuBois was well thought of in the community, and the funeral was well attended, including a large contingent of Omaha Police Officers.[583]

Prior to Sam DuBois' funeral on the 16th of December, Sheriff John Drexel was called upon, because of the absence of Acting Coroner Mike Maul, to perform the duty of presiding at a coroner's inquest to consider the death of DuBois. Several witnesses were called and examined by assistant County Attorney Sam Winters. The coroner's jury quickly rendered its verdict by saying that the death of DuBois was caused from the "effects of pistol shots," and subsequent wounds which were caused by, "Claude Henry Hoover, fired with felonious intent." Claude Hoover was not present at the inquest.[584] On the 18th of December, Hoover appeared with his attorney, Mr. Powers, at a preliminary hearing.

The defense offered no testimony or opposition. The news accounts noted that Hoover, "presented the appearance of a man who was without a friend in the world and without hope of a brilliant future staring him in the face."[585] On the 24th of December, 1895, Christmas Eve, information was filed by County Attorney H. H. Baldridge charging Hoover with murder. In Nebraska, the filing of information was a substitute for a grand jury proceeding.[586]

On Thursday the 26th of December, ten days after the funeral of DuBois and the coroner's inquest, the trial of Claude Hoover began in District Court. Two motions were filed on behalf of Hoover before the trial judge, Cunningham R. Scott.[587] The attorneys representing Hoover and presenting the motions in Hoover's behalf were James A. Powers and M. C. Acheson. The first was a technical issue involving a word which had been altered in the information, and the second was to quash the information based upon the fact that the defense did not have sufficient time to prepare their case. Judge Scott ruled against both motions from the bench and the trial commenced. The balance of the day on the 26th was spent selecting the jury.[588]

On the morning of the 27th, the State presented several witnesses, including the doctors who initially attended DuBois. Hoover's stepsister testified concerning the first altercation, and the witnesses from the shoe store testified that they actually saw Hoover shoot DuBois. The State's case was concluded at 2:00 P.M.[589]

The defense's case was based solely on the fact that Hoover was intoxicated at the time of the act and therefore insane when the shooting occurred. Dubois's widow, Hoover's sister, was called and was asked questions concerning her brother's sanity. Katie Brophy, Hoover's stepsister, was re-called to the stand and asked similar questions. The majority of questions asked were objected to by Mr. Baldridge. Most were ruled inadmissible by Judge Scott on the basis that they called for conclusions from the witnesses. The defense rested its case at 3:15 P.M. The balance of the day was given to both attorneys for submitting their arguments to the jury.[590] On the following day, Saturday the 28th of December, trial continued with the final summation of the state's case and the charging of the jury by Judge Scott. The jury was given the case on Saturday morning at 11:30 A.M.[591]

On Sunday morning, the 29th of December, the jury announced it had reached a verdict. The Judge, the defendant, and all other trial participants were assembled by 10:30 A.M. to hear the verdict. The foreman of the jury handed the written verdict to the judge, who then asked the clerk to read the verdict out loud. In a clear voice, he said, "We the jury impaneled and sworn do find the defendant, Claude H. Hoover, guilty of the crime of murder in the first degree as charged in the second count of the information, and we determine that said defendant shall suffer death."[592]

On January 3, 1896, Judge Scott entertained a motion for a new trial from attorneys Powers and Acheson on behalf of Hoover. Mr. Powers argued that additional evidence with respect to the intoxicated condition of Hoover at the time of the incident could be provided in the form of testimony of his stepfather. After listening to all of the arguments, Judge Scott rendered a decision not to grant a new trial. He then addressed Hoover by first recapping his crime and then set the date of April 17, 1896 as the date that Hoover was to go to the gallows.

On February 11, 1896, attorneys for Hoover filed an affidavit of poverty hoping to get Hoover's case heard by Nebraska's Supreme Court.[593] On February 19, 1896, the Clerk of the Nebraska Supreme Court accepted the appeal and supporting briefs from Hoover's attorneys and filed his appeal with the Court.[594] There was little for attorneys Powers and Acheson to argue. The court considered several technical errors involving the wording of the information and the fact that non-expert witnesses commented on Hoover's sanity. The court found no validity in any of the arguments.[595]

On April 21, the Nebraska Supreme Court rendered its decision and said, "The verdict is sustained by ample evidence, which was uncontradicted, and the judgment of the district court thereon is affirmed." The court also noted in their order that the sentence was to be carried out on August 7, 1896.[596] Two Justices, Irvine and Regan, both dissented in the opinion agreeing with the defense attorneys that they did not have enough time to prepare an adequate defense.[597] Based upon the fact that there was a dissent, on May 5, 1896, the attorneys asked the Court for a rehearing asking them to again consider the fact that Hoover's trial was too expeditious. They stressed the fact that they were both appointed by the District Court, that the complaint was not served until the afternoon of December 24, 1895, that the following day was Christmas, and the trial began on December 26, the day after Christmas. For this reason, they argued, they were not afforded ample opportunity to prepare a defense for Hoover.[598]

On June 3, 1896, the Supreme Court answered and refused Hoover a rehearing.[599]

On July 13, 1896, attorneys Acheson and Powers along with Claude Hoover's mother and half-sister went to Lincoln to see Governor Silas Holcomb to plead for Hoover's life. The attorneys had previously filed an application asking the governor to commute the sentence to life imprisonment. The attorneys carried with them a petition signed by several attorneys saying the trial was too quick.[600] On August 3, 1895, the governor made his intentions clear that he would not interfere with the Court's mandate to proceed with Hoover's execution, and also sent a note to Douglas County Sheriff John McDonald to that effect.[601] The governor waited until the day before the scheduled execution to end all speculation that he may make the commutation when he responded to a final appeal from two additional Omaha attorneys, Kaley and Simeral. In a telegram on August 6, 1896, Holcomb said, "Sentiment only exists for executive interference. I cannot act on that."[602]

On August 4, after receiving the telegram, Sheriff McDonald began the necessary preparations for carrying out the execution. He made arrangements to construct the required stockade fence near the southwest corner of the jail yard, which would hide the execution from public view, and saw to it, according to the *Omaha Daily Bee*, that the "work of erecting the engine of death will be commenced in the morning."[603] By the evening of August 6, 1896, all of the construction was completed, and the apparatus dubbed by the *Omaha Daily Bee* as the "engine of death" had been tested and found to be working perfectly.[604] Sheriff McDonald had an additional button added to the gallows after the Dixon execution, which allowed 4 persons instead of 3 to simultaneously press them. On August 6, M. C. Acheson, one of Hoover's attorneys made public that he would be presenting a statement on behalf of Hoover, saying, "as soon the breath is out of Hoover's body, he would have a statement to make."[605]

About 11:15 A.M. on the 7th of August, 1896, Sheriff McDonald, with a contingent of his deputies, went into the jail and then directly to Hoover's cell. The sheriff then read the death warrant to Hoover while Hoover stood motionless and listened. The warrant ordered that the sheriff, "On the seventh day of August in the year of our Lord 1896," to, "take the said Claude H. Hoover to a place prepared in Douglas County, in the State of Nebraska, and in there to hang him, the said Claude H. Hoover, by the neck until dead."[606] During the reading, it was apparent to the bystanders that it was a very unpleasant task for the sheriff.[607]

As soon as the warrant was read, the sheriff, Hoover, attorney Powers, and the rest of the contingent, with Hoover in the middle, began their walk through the jail and into the yard. In a very businesslike manner, they ascended the steps of the scaffold. Attorney Powers was allowed to make a statement concerning the facts of the case and gave a recap of the legal proceedings. He then, to the surprise of some, read a letter from the condemned Hoover in which Hoover confessed to the crime. At the end, he added that it was the alcohol that caused him to take the life of DuBois and deprive his sister of a husband and their children of a father. Hoover was allowed to make a last statement. He said that he had no malice or bore no ill will to anyone, and finished by saying, "God bless you all," and, "I am ready."[608] At that point, it was the Reverend J. M. Wilson's turn to conduct the religious ceremony with prayers and a Presbyterian benediction.[609]

At the close of the prayer, Sheriff McDonald stepped forward and placed the black cap over the head of Hoover, who had previously been bound at the arms, knees, and ankles by his deputies. The sheriff placed the noose around his neck, and stepped back. At 11:36 A.M., the buttons were pressed and the trap door was sprung, sending Hoover to his death. At 11:50 A.M., Hoover was pronounced dead. His body hung under the gallows for another seven minutes until it was cut down and turned over to the coroner.[610]

Hoover's body was released and subsequently taken to the home of his mother and sister, who were living at 3197 South 13th Street, the residence of Sam DuBois. Hoover's funeral was held on Sunday, August 9, at 2:30 P.M. at the Castelar Presbyterian Church. The Reverend J. M. Wilson officiated over the funeral and read a sermon written by Hoover on the subject of intemperance.[611]

In addition to both Hoover's wake and DuBois funeral being held at the same residence, another bit of irony was that Hoover, like DuBois, was buried at Laurel Hill Cemetery. The records of the cemetery do not indicate where Hoover was buried.[612] The last irony is that Hoover, like Ed Neal, was destined to spend eternity in an unmarked grave, probably for the same reason as Neal. John Sautter, the owner of Laurel Hill Cemetery found it necessary to hire watchmen to guard the resting place of Claude H. Hoover because it was feared that "an attempt would be made to rob the grave." Sautter said that he would post the guard as long as "there was a danger of the ghouls making any attempt to steal the remains."[613]

An interesting post script to the Hoover case comes as the story of Reverend Charles W. Savidge. After Hoover's execution, the Reverend began a movement to reach and reform the derelicts of the community. His method was to hold regular weekly meetings at which he re-told the story of Hoover's life, crime, and unfortunate end. His efforts eventually earned him statewide recognition through his preaching against the evils of drink.[614]

Sheriff John Drexel

Claude Hoover

Sam DuBois

Chapter XIII
George Morgan
Child Molester

Eleven year old Ida Gaskill lived with her mother and ten year old brother in downtown Omaha. Her father died when she and her brother were very young. Her widowed mother, Mary Gaskill, worked very hard to raise her two children. She worked all day at what was commonly referred to as a "steam laundry." Ida was described by a reporter for the *Evening World Herald* as being, "the chubby, blonde haired and blue-eyed daughter of a poor widow living at 1814 Half-Howard Street."[615] A reporter for the *Omaha Daily Bee* described her as having, "an extremely pretty face, and lovely hair."[616] On Sunday evening, November 3, 1895, little Ida Gaskill died. She lost her innocence and her life in a very violent manner.[617]

The Gaskill family lived on the third floor of an apartment building in downtown Omaha. Mrs. Gaskill befriended a man named Martin Booker who worked as a coal hauler. Booker lived at 1808 Saint Mary's Avenue, which was just around the corner from the Gaskill's. Booker and the Gaskill family socialized frequently, usually by sharing meals together. Around 4:30 in the afternoon on Sunday, November 3, 1895, Mrs. Gaskill sent Ida to Booker's apartment with a message to invite him to supper. Mrs. Gaskill, like any mother, began worrying when Ida did not return from her errand. She also thought it odd that Booker didn't immediately accept the invitation. He rarely turned down her home cooked meals, and because it was uncharacteristic for him, she was worried. Mrs. Gaskill became more anxious as the hours passed. By 11:00 P.M. she knew something must be seriously wrong and notified Omaha police.[618]

Detective Hudson was given the assignment to find Ida. He quickly arranged a search of the neighborhood, and was joined by other police officers. All involved were intent on finding little Ida, but it was Detective McGrath who made the gruesome discovery. Several officers entered an abandoned ten room house referred to as a "shanty," but it was McGrath who looked in a closet in a room on the first floor. It was there he found little Ida's dead body. McGrath suspected immediately that she had been the victim of a murder and sexual assault. Her clothes were in disarray and in an awkward position on her body.[619] Her undergarments had been ripped from her body and her lower extremities were smeared with blood. It was also immediately apparent to the detective that Ida was the victim of strangulation.[620] The body showed, "well-defined finger marks on the larynx," and "also below the left ear and under the chin."[621]

The detectives hastily went to work trying to find Ida's killer. The most obvious suspect was Martin Booker, who was picked up and whisked off to the police station for questioning.[622] Police officers were methodical in their investigation, and quickly found another promising suspect who lived in Ida's apartment building. Two single men shared adjoining rooms in an apartment located on the first floor. When police officers knocked on the door, they found Ed Sanford alone in his room. It was apparent to police that Sanford had been sleeping when they finally were able to rouse him. In an adjoining room they found George Morgan, who also appeared to have been sleeping. The detectives quickly determined Morgan was their prime suspect because they found incriminating evidence in his room.[623] "His trousers were smeared with blood on the front, and his lower shirt front was spotted with blood, there were traces of blood on his left-hand and on his coat was completely filled with dust on the back(sic)."[624] Both Morgan and Sanford were taken in for questioning.

At Morgan's initial interview he openly admitted seeing little Ida on the afternoon of her death. Morgan said Ida asked him if he had seen Martin Booker, and told him she had a message for Booker. Morgan related that he told Ida that if he saw him, he would relate the message that Booker was to come to supper. Morgan continued saying that he even went to Booker's office but found no one there, so he went back to his room. Morgan told detectives that when he got back to his room, he drank and played cards with Sanford and two other men.[625] Morgan was asked about the bloodstains. He was perplexed and said that he didn't know how he got them. Sanford's story seemed to support Morgan's alibi, but Sanford told authorities that Morgan left the card game for an hour or so shortly after dark. He said Morgan was unaccounted for during that time, but added that Morgan eventually returned home and went to bed.[626]

The police continued their investigation and interviewed Willie Gaskill, Ida's ten year old brother. He told officers that he saw

Morgan in the vacant house where Ida's body was found around 4:00 P.M. on the afternoon of the murder. Willie's first story to police was that Morgan asked him to tell Ida that he (Morgan) wanted to send her on an errand.[627] Subsequently, the boy told police that Morgan paid him to tell Ida that he wanted her to meet him in the abandoned house. Willie also said that he delivered the message to Ida and then returned to the abandoned house and told Morgan that his sister was given the message. During this conversation, Willie asked Morgan why he was hiding in the old house, and Morgan replied angrily that he wasn't hiding. Morgan gave Willie a penny to buy some taffy. As Willie was returning home he met Ida on her way out the door. He asked where she was going and she replied that she was delivering a message to Martin Booker.[628]

As the investigation continued, Morgan maintained that he knew nothing of the killing. A search of his room found a handkerchief soaked in blood, and when Morgan was confronted with the evidence, he said that the blood on his clothing and the handkerchief were a result of him coming in contact with a side of beef he was lugging while working for a neighborhood butcher. He continued by saying he was drunk that afternoon and could not recall everything that happened while he was in that condition.[629] He openly admitted that he was an ex-convict who spent eighteen months in the Nebraska Penitentiary after being convicted of burglary. Morgan also admitted that he had been previously arrested in Blair, Nebraska and charged with molesting a young girl. Morgan related that he was acquitted at trial, because the state could not prove injury to the child.[630] A Blair, Nebraska merchant, who said he was well acquainted with Morgan, told the newspapers that Morgan had served time at the penitentiary in Joliet, Illinois for stealing horses and that his true name was actually Nelson B. Morgan.[631] He also said that Morgan had a wife and children in Champaign, Illinois.[632]

Captain King and all of the other detectives handling the case were confident that Morgan was Ida's killer, and they moved quickly to arrest him on murder charges. Morgan was taken to the county jail, and Sanford, based upon the fact that the police believed he was not complicit in the death, was released.[633]

Ida's body was examined at the morgue by Dr. Rebert, and then, as was the custom of the day, covered with a sheet and put on display for the public view. So many people came to view the body that it was necessary for her to be moved to the basement simply to accommodate the ingress and egress of the large number of people wanting to see her. It was estimated that, "the body was viewed by thousands of men, women, and children."[634] After a few hours the procession stopped, and a crowd began to gather in front of the morgue. Authorities began worrying about a lynching. It was decided that Morgan should be taken to the penitentiary in Lincoln. Sheriff Drexel, with the help of some deputy U. S. marshal's, took Morgan to the train station. The lawmen and their suspect were followed by several people to the depot, and a large crowd soon gathered and began clamoring, "Lynch the murderer."[635] With the help of several Omaha police officers, the group was able to board the train and leave for Lincoln without further incident.[636] Meanwhile, while Morgan was being moved to Lincoln, a crowd began gathering near the courthouse and the jail. The group was told that Morgan was no longer there, but the mob continued to grow. Over one hundred deputies and police officers were called to the scene to maintain order. Between late Monday afternoon and evening, several persons were arrested on charges of disturbing the peace and inciting a riot, but by 9:30 P.M. the crowd had been effectively dispersed.[637]

On Wednesday, November 6th, 1895, a funeral was held for little Ida Gaskill at Kountze Memorial Lutheran Church, which at the time, was located at 16th and Harney Streets in downtown Omaha.[638] The church was completely filled with mourners, including Ida's entire Sunday School class. The service was conducted by Reverend Alonzo Turkle, who delivered a very emotional eulogy in which he mentioned the crime that took Ida's life. He said Ida died, "in an attempt to protect her honor at the hands of a fiend in human form."[639] The depravity of the crime and the fact the Gaskill family was poor, spurred the businessmen of Omaha to collect a dollar from each of them to defray Ida's mother's funeral costs. The collection raised seventy-one dollars. Ida was buried and is still at rest in Omaha's Forrest Lawn Cemetery under a marker depicting her resemblance.[640]

County Attorney H. H. Baldridge was in-charge of the prosecution of Morgan. At the time, the law required that a preliminary hearing be held within a very short time of the arrest unless the requirement was waived by the defendant. In this case it made it more difficult for Baldridge because of the volatile feelings of the public and the near riot on the night of his arrest. Baldridge also had a logistical problem because Morgan was being held in Lincoln. The county attorney made a public statement that he would return Morgan in the middle of the night, hold the preliminary hearing, and then immediately have him taken back to Lincoln.[641] Baldridge brought back Morgan on November 17th, a week after his comments to the press. Newspapers reported that the hearing was delayed due to Baldridge's absence from the city. At the hearing, Morgan waived his right to a preliminary hearing, and the case was headed for trial.[642] On November 23, 1895, Morgan appeared in Douglas County District Court and entered a plea of "not guilty" to two charges. The judge appointed two attorneys to represent him.[643]

The trial of Nelson W. (George) Morgan began on Friday the 29th of November 1895 in front of Judge Cunningham R. Scott. The attorney of record for the state was County Attorney H. H. Baldridge, and attorneys W. R. Patrick and R. B. Montgomery represented Morgan. It took all day Friday and the first half of Saturday to seat a twelve man jury. The trial was scheduled to begin with opening arguments on Monday morning, December 2nd.[644]

Baldridge's opening remarks simply covered the facts surrounding Ida's death and the circumstantial evidence the police gathered pointing to Morgan as the killer. Baldridge emphasized the fact that when Morgan was awakened by police, he had blood on the front of his shirt, his trousers, and under his fingernails. He also mentioned the fact that the officers had found bloody fingerprints on the wash bowl purportedly used by Morgan. Patrick's comments simply cautioned the jury to pay particular attention to the evidence presented by the prosecution.[645]

The state's first witness was Dr. Rebert, who testified concerning his post mortem examination of Ida's body. He also provided the foundation necessary for the introduction of photographs showing the little girl's injuries taken at the morgue. The police photographer then testified to taking pictures at the crime scene. The photographs were admitted into evidence and handed to the jury. According to reporters, each juror showed a strong reaction when they looked at the pictures.[646] The state's case continued with the calling of several more witnesses, including several police officers. The cross-examination by defense attorneys led to questions implying that the police ended their investigation too soon, and it culminated with the arrest of Morgan.[647]

The following day, the State's case continued with the testimony of Ida's little brother, who re-told his story of seeing Morgan in the vacant house where the crime occurred. He was also very detailed when telling how Morgan sent him with a message for his sister. On cross-examination, the defense attorney made Willie repeat his story several times in an attempt to get him to waiver from the story he first gave to police and then repeated on the witness stand. Attorney Patrick did not succeed in his attempt to confuse the child, but did manage to make the boy cry. The state then called Ida's mother, who essentially testified to the fact that she sent Ida to Booker's and then became anguished when she did not return.[648]

The state originally subpoenaed sixty-two witnesses.[649] On the third day of testimony, it was decided that the state had exhausted all of its direct evidence. Based upon the large number of subpoenas issued, the defense team was not ready to begin examining defense witnesses. They asked Judge Scott for a few additional hours so they could contact witnesses and prepare the case. Judge Scott denied their request and ordered the trial to resume. The defense put on a few witnesses that seemed to provide an alibi for Morgan, but the veracity of the evidence was challenged by Judge Scott. Eventually, the defense decided to put Morgan on the stand.[650]

Morgan's testimony was tedious, and he spent a great deal of time reciting his history and how he ended up in Nebraska. He admitted being in prison in both Illinois and Nebraska. He also admitted being charged and tried in the kidnapping case in Blair. After some time, he moved his testimony towards Booker, with the inference that it was Booker who had more of an opportunity to kill Ida than he did. The testimony regarding Booker was inferential, and he made his point without actually accusing him. Morgan again mentioned that the blood probably came from the fact that he worked for a butcher and was lugging beef the day before the murder. He also remembered waking up from a sound sleep because his nose was bleeding. He said he remembered wiping his nose with his hand, which accounted for the blood police found on his hands. As far as the wash bowl was concerned, he recalled cleaning fish near the bowl and getting blood from the fish on the bowl.[651] The blood evidence and Morgan's subsequent explanations became a critical part of the state's case.

Deputy County Attorney Slabaugh cross examined Morgan but was unable to get an admission or shake Morgan's testimony. Judge Scott stopped Slabaugh at one point when he asked Morgan questions about the Blair incident, and ruled that the event was not to be used in connection with the case at trial. The state then called several witnesses in rebuttal to the story told by Morgan, including the owner of the butcher shop, who testified that Morgan did not handle any meat on the day in question, but he added that he could have brushed up against a piece of hanging beef and got blood on this clothes.[652] The state then called Booker to the stand in an attempt to eliminate the suggestions that he was in fact the killer. Booker testified to his whereabouts during the entire evening. Next, the State called witnesses who verified Booker's statements.[653]

The case continued on Saturday with lengthy closing arguments on both sides, and early in the evening, the case went to the jury.[654] The jury was out until Sunday morning and reached a verdict at approximately 9:00 A.M. By 11:00 A.M., Judge Scott and the jury were ready to act on the verdict. The judge summoned all of the attorneys to his courtroom shortly after he was notified that the jury reached a decision. By 11:00 A.M., Judge Scott had waited long enough and decided to take the verdict without the presence of the lawyers for either side.[655] Judge Scott asked the jury, "Gentlemen, have you decided on a verdict?" A. C. Woody, jury foreman, answered, "We have." Clerk Frank E. Moores was handed the verdict and read it out loud. "We the jury duly impaneled and sworn do find the defendant, George Morgan, not guilty of the crime charged in the first count of the information, and find him guilty of murder in the first degree in manner and form as charged in the second count of the information, and we do determine that the defendant shall suffer death."[656] Judge Scott then took it upon himself to poll the jury. Each member voiced their guilty verdict, and asserted in a clear voice that it was "still his verdict."[657]

On Saturday, December 21, 1895, Morgan was back in court before Judge Scott with his attorneys Patrick and Montgomery. Patrick presented the judge with a motion in the form of an affidavit asking the judge for a new trial on the basis of improper jury selection. Judge Scott unleashed a furious verbal attack on Patrick, saying that he took the motion as a "personal affront." He continued by saying that Patrick thanked the court for conducting a "fair and impartial trial" in open court, and could not understand why the attorney would go back on his word. Next, it was Mr. Montgomery's turn to present additional motions asking for a new trial on several other grounds, including errors made by the court. Judge Scott began his censure by addressing Montgomery, "You, under your oath, declared in open court that no case was more fairly tried, and now you come here to make these charges."[658] After the lengthy tongue lashing of the two attorneys, Judge Scott abruptly ruled against all of the motions and denied a new trial. He then summoned Morgan to the bench.

Judge Scott calmly told Morgan that his crime was, "unparalleled in its heinousness," and that everyone was, "aghast at the spectacle of a man committing murder for his purpose of gratifying his lust upon a child." Judge Scott then pronounced that he would be, "hanged by the sheriff of Douglas County on Friday, April 17, 1896."[659]

Morgan's attorney R. B. Montgomery publicly announced that he would not pursue an appeal of Judge Scott's ruling to the Supreme Court. However, W. R. Patrick apparently decided that an appeal was in order and publicly stated that he would seek funds to create a transcript of the trial in order that an appeal could be made.[660] On January 22, 1896, Patrick asked the Supreme Court to order Judge Scott to have a handwritten transcript made of the trial.[661] On April 7, 1896, just days before his scheduled execution, the Supreme Court issued a stay and decided to review Morgan's case.[662] The wrangling over the payment of the transcript continued in the Supreme Court.[663] The effect of the contention kept Morgan's appeal from being heard through the court's summer break and into a new court calendar. The appeal of Morgan's case to the Supreme Court contained several issues, but the most important was the sufficiency of the circumstantial evidence to convict. After several months, the court finally rendered its decision on June 3, 1897. The court in effect denied a new trial and affirmed the decision of the lower court.[664] Morgan's execution was set for October 8, 1897.[665] Morgan's attorney, W. R. Patrick, filed an application with the court for a rehearing shortly after the decision. The Supreme Court adjourned before taking any action on Patrick's motion. It was scheduled to reconvene on October 5, 1897, which was only three days before the scheduled execution.[666]

Sheriff McDonald was once again faced with the task of preparing for a hanging, but he first wanted to determine the likelihood of the execution actually taking place. He set up a meeting with the clerk of the Supreme Court, who outlined the process and indicated that the execution would more than likely go ahead as scheduled. After hearing this news, he paid a visit to Governor Holcomb. Shortly after returning to Omaha, he began making preparations to build a stockade enclosure on the west side of the courthouse to hide the execution from the public.[667] Once the stockade was completed, it was time to erect the now famous "death machine." The *Omaha Daily Bee* reported the details of the construction. "Yesterday afternoon the scaffold upon which the convicted murderer will be hanged was put in place. It is the same upon which Hoover was hanged last year, with the exception that a new beam has been put in to replace one that was broken. It is given a new coat of black paint. The machine has been raised about a foot and a half higher than it was when Hoover occupied it, as Morgan is considerably taller. The machine was tested in the afternoon."[668]

On October 6, 1897, the Supreme Court ruled against Morgan and denied him a rehearing. Thinking the court would not rule in time, Morgan's attorneys had previously made a preemptive plea to Governor Holcomb for clemency. That request was denied. After the court's ruling of October 6th, the governor was asked a second time to reduce Morgan's sentence to life, but he once again refused to spare his life. Shortly after the last denial, the governor left the State and traveled to Tarkio, Missouri on State business.[669] James E Harris, Nebraska's lieutenant governor, was already out of the State in Tarkio at the same meeting as the governor. In the absence of both of these men, the acting governor of the State was Frank T. Ransom, President Pro Tem of the Nebraska Legislature. When Governor Holcomb left on his trip, he provided Ransom a letter indicating that both he and the lieutenant governor would be absent from the State. The letter also mentioned that there was no "executive business that was likely to come up," but continued as if to say coincidentally, "you will be applied to for a reprieve of George W. Morgan."[670] Morgan's attorneys contacted Ransom and made a final appeal, but he refused to consider it.[671] Ransom would later say that he did not even consider issuing a reprieve as it would have been contrary to Governor Holcomb's decision.[672] Sheriff McDonald was in possession of the death warrant, and Morgan's execution was cleared of all stops.

October 8, 1897 was not an ordinary day at the Douglas County Jail. Sheriff McDonald and several additional deputies were there early. The sheriff himself and a few of his key personnel spent the night at the jail in anticipation of the impending execution.[673] Father Peters of Creighton University, who had become Morgan's religious counsel, was also up early to meet with Morgan. After they prayed, Father Peters left, but then returned around 9:00 A.M. in the company of Father Barrett of St. Philomena's Cathedral, who had agreed to conduct the last rites for Morgan. At 11:18 A.M., Sheriff McDonald and several of his deputies went to Morgan's cell to read the death warrant and escort Morgan to the gallows. The sheriff began by saying, "It is my painful duty to read the following," and then the sheriff read the warrant out loud. A minute later the sheriff, deputies, the two priests, and Morgan began the walk to the stockade located on the west side of the courthouse.[674]

The procession reached the scaffold and Morgan ascended the stairs and stood on the trap door. Morgan then prayed with Fathers Peters and Barrett. After the priests were done, Sheriff McDonald asked Morgan if he had anything to say. Morgan said yes and stepped forward towards the railing.[675] Morgan addressed the crowd and basically talked of his conversion to Catholicism. He made no mention of the crime for which he was convicted and showed no remorse for taking the life of the little girl.[676] At the conclusion of his speech, he made several comments about his soul, and while sobbing, said goodbye to his attorney, Mr. Patrick, who was in the small crowd of onlookers. A singular response from the crowd was a faint, "goodbye George."[677]

Morgan then stepped back onto the trap door, and deputies quickly bound his arms, wrists, and knees. They placed a noose around Morgan's neck and cinched it into place. Next, they slipped a black cap over his head and stepped away. The signal was given, and shortly after at 11:34 A.M. deputies pressed the electric buttons, one of which released the trapdoor, allowing Morgan to drop to his death.[678] Deputy Sheriff John Lewis grabbed Morgan's body to prevent it from swinging. "There was not a motion of the limbs after the trap had been sprung there was none of the twitching and drawing up of the legs which usually follow after the drop."[679] Morgan was pronounced dead at 11:44 A.M.[680]

J. A. Taggert, owner of Taggert's Undertaking Parlor, located at 23rd and Cuming Streets, took charge of Morgan's body after it was removed from the gallows. The body was put on public display from early afternoon until Friday evening. A "constant stream of on lookers," stopped to view the body."[681] Morgan's body was later shipped to his family in Champaign, Illinois for burial.[682]

The two newspapers of the day, *The Omaha Daily Bee* and *The Evening World Herald*, carried contradicting stories concerning purported confessions made by Morgan before he went to his death. The significance of the controversy was the question of Morgan's guilt. If Morgan had confessed, then his guilt would no longer be an issue. The legitimate legal basis for Morgan's appeal, according to his attorney, was that he was solely convicted based upon circumstantial evidence. That left room for some skeptics.

The *Evening World Herald* reported that Morgan made no less than three confessions to his crime. The first came within forty-eight hours and was made to an attorney, who at the time was considering representing him. The attorney simply asked Morgan if he had committed the crime, to which he replied that he did. The attorney, who subsequently did not represent Morgan, purportedly divulged this information to Deputy County Attorney Slabaugh.[683] The news account reported that Deputy John Kenworthy, who worked on Morgan's "death watch," was taken into Morgan's confidence approximately two weeks prior to the execution. Morgan supposedly told Kenworthy that he killed Ida, and provided him with specific details.[684] The reports concerning the confessions concluded with a story that Sheriff McDonald was summoned to Morgan's cell on the night before the execution for a lengthy confidential discussion. When reporters asked the sheriff if the purpose of the visit was Morgan's confession, he would not confirm it or deny it leading to speculation that it was a confession.[685]

The following day, *The Omaha Daily Bee* carried a story that challenged the earlier report. John Kenworthy was said to deny that Morgan had confessed, but added that based upon a series of discussions he had with Morgan over several months, he had no doubt of Morgan's guilt. Sheriff McDonald told the paper, "Morgan never said a word to him which could be construed as being an acknowledgment of his guilt."[686]

Sheriff McDonald, for the second time, was asked to carry out the duties of executing a prisoner, and did so in an extremely professional manner. He left the "death machine" in place and open to public inspection over the weekend, and then had it disassembled and stored for the next time.[687]

Sheriff John McDonald

George W. Morgan

Headstone - Ida Gaskill

Chapter XIV
3980

When Douglas County Sheriff John McDonald presided over the execution of George Morgan, it was the first time a Nebraska county sheriff had the distasteful task of consecutively hanging two men. Dodge County Sheriff James Milliken hung two men, but did it simultaneously. Custer County Sheriff "Big Jim" Jones hung one man twice. Otoe County Sheriff George MaCallum and Cass County Sheriff J. C. Eikenbary each hung one man, but most said the sheriffs should have hung two. The Morgan hanging also had another historical distinction. When Sheriff McDonald ordered the scaffold, which had earned the colorful sobriquet "the death machine," dismantled and stored, it was the last gallows used by a Nebraska sheriff to preside over an execution. In 1901, a law passed by the Nebraska Legislature mandated all executions be conducted under the auspices of the warden at the Nebraska Penitentiary.[688] The policy change, however, did not completely end the involvement of the Douglas County Sheriff.

Gottlieb Neigenfind was convicted in Pierce County for going on a shooting rampage and killing his father-in-law and estranged wife.[689] In March of 1903, Warden Allen D. Beemer of Nebraska's penitentiary had to figure out a way to hang Neigenfind, so he tapped the expertise of Douglas County. The Warden decided to ask Douglas County's Sheriff, John Power, for help. After all, at that time, Douglas County was more experienced than he or anyone else in the State with the business of hanging people. After some discussion, between the Warden and Douglas County Officials, the Wednesday, March 4th edition of the *Evening World Herald* carried the headline, "County Would Sell Its Death Machine."[690] The plan seemed to be a practical solution for both parties involved. Douglas County had a modern gallows, in perfect condition, equipped with the latest electrical trap door, and only used sparingly. It was just sitting in the basement of the Courthouse gathering dust. What's more, the Legislature had made the machine obsolete as far as they were concerned. On the other hand, the Warden was in need of a scaffold, and in a hurry. The parties agreed on the price of fifty dollars, and Douglas

County sold the machine with all of its "ghastly accoutrements" to the State, including the "black cap."[691] The machine was shipped on Tuesday March 10, 1903. The execution was scheduled for Friday the 13th of March, just 3 days later. Sheriff Power agreed to personally oversee the delivery of the machine and help the warden set it up.[692] The warden also asked for the help of Sheriff McDonald because of his recent experience operating the machine, but news reports indicated that he did not know if he would be able to attend.[693]

On March 11, 1903, Governor Mickey refused a plea of clemency for Gottlieb Neigenfind, designated Nebraska penitentiary inmate #3980.[694] The headlines in the October 19, 1903 edition of *Custer County Republican* read, "Gottlieb Neigenfind Dons the Black Cap and Maintains Stoicism to the Last."[695] The State of Nebraska would use the death machine seven more times before 1913.[696] In that year, the Legislature adopted the language; "to be electrocuted by the passage of electric current through his body until dead"[697] The statute ended capital punishment by hanging in Nebraska.

Gottleib Neigenfind
Courtesy of Nebraska Department of Corrections

Sheriff John Power

1 *The Omaha Daily Bee*; Sunday, August 25, 1889

2 *The Omaha Daily Bee*; Sunday, August 25, 1889

3   History of Richardson County, Nebraska; Lewis Edwards; B. F. Bowen; Indianapolis, 1917

4   History of Richardson County, Nebraska; Lewis Edwards; B. F. Bowen; Indianapolis, 1917

5 *The Omaha Daily Bee*; January 13, 1887

6 *Omaha Daily Herald*; July 25, 1887

7 *Omaha Daily Herald*; April 30, 1886

8 *McCook Tribune*; May 13, 1886

9 *The Omaha Sunday Bee*; July 24, 1887

10 *The Omaha Daily Bee*; July 25, 1887

11 *Omaha Daily Herald*; July 25, 1887

12 *The Omaha Daily Bee*; July 25, 1887

13 *Morning World Herald*; October 10, 1891

14 *The Omaha Daily Bee*; October 11, 1891

15 *Morning World-Herald*; October 10, 1891

16 *The Omaha Daily Bee*; October 11, 1891

17 *The Omaha Daily Bee*; October 10, 1891

18 *Morning World-Herald*; October 10, 1891

19 *The Omaha Daily Bee;* October 11, 1891

20 *The Omaha Daily Bee;* October 11, 1891

21   *The Daily Nebraska State Journal;* Saturday, July 25, 1885 & *The Omaha Daily Bee;* October 11, 1891

22 *Omaha Daily Herald*; July 25, 1887

23 *Omaha World-Herald*; March 15, 1895

24 *Evening World Herald*; March 6, 1895

25 *The Evening World-Herald*, March 7 & 28, 1895

26   On October 19, 1903, Gottlieb Neigenfind was the first prisoner executed at the Nebraska Penitentiary

27   Wearing the Hempen Necktie: Lynching in Nebraska, 1858-1919; James E. Potter; *Nebraska History*; Fall, 2012; p. 138-153

28   *Omaha Evening News*; April 26, 1879

29 *Omaha Herald*; April 27, 1879

30   *The Nemaha Advertiser*, January 2, 1879; & Happy as a Big Sunflower; Rolf Johnson, Editor , Richard Jensen; University of Nebraska Press, 2000, pp. 138-152

31   History of Omaha from the Pioneer Days to the Present; A. Sorenson; Gibson-Miller Printers; Omaha; 1889 p. 130

32   *Hastings Gazette*; April 26, 1879 & Happy as a Big Sunflower; Rolf Johnson, Editor , Richard Jensen; University of Nebraska Press, 2000, pp. 138-152

33 *Omaha Daily Republican*; April 27, 1879

34   Happy as a Big Sunflower; Rolf Johnson, Editor , Richard Jensen; University of Nebraska Press, 2000, p. 138

35 *Omaha World-Herald*; September 27, 1953

36   *The Red Cloud Chief*; May 15, 1879, & Heroes Without Medals: A Pioneer History of Kearney County Nebraska; Roy C. Bang; Warp Publishing; Minden, Nebraska; 1952

37   Heroes Without Medals: A Pioneer History of Kearney County Nebraska; Roy C. Bang; Warp Publishing; Minden, Nebraska; 1952

38   *The Columbus Journal*; July 23, 1879 & *Nemaha Advertiser;* July 24, 1879

39   Heroes Without Medals: A Pioneer History of Kearney County Nebraska; Roy C. Bang; Warp Publishing; Minden, Nebraska; 1952

40   S. D. Richard's background comes from *Omaha Evening News*; April 26, 1879; The *Omaha Daily Republican*; April 27, 1879; & Richard's complied confessions to several newspapers and reported collectively in Happy as a Big Sunflower; Rolf Johnson, Editor , Richard Jensen; University of Nebraska Press, 2000

41   Happy as a Big Sunflower; Rolf Johnson, Editor , Richard Jensen; University of Nebraska Press, 2000; & The *Omaha Daily Republican*; April 27, 1879

42 *Omaha Evening News*; April 26, 1879

43   Empire on the Platte; Richard Crabb; World Publishing; New York & Cleveland; 1967

44   Happy as a Big Sunflower; Rolf Johnson, Editor , Richard Jensen; University of Nebraska Press, 2000

45   Happy as a Big Sunflower; Rolf Johnson, Editor , Richard Jensen; University of Nebraska Press, 2000

46   Happy as a Big Sunflower; Rolf Johnson, Editor , Richard Jensen; University of Nebraska Press, 2000

47 *Omaha Daily Republican*; April 27, 1879

48   Happy as a Big Sunflower; Rolf Johnson, Editor , Richard Jensen; University of Nebraska Press, 2000

49   *Nebraska Advertiser;* September 27; 1877 & Historical Atlas of the Outlaw West; Richard Patterson; Johnson Publishing; Boulder, Co; 1985 & *Nebraska Advertiser;* September 27; 1877

50   *Nebraska Advertiser*; January 2, 1879 & The Omaha Daily Bee; April 18, 1882 & *Omaha World Herald*; June 1, 1998

51   Happy as a Big Sunflower; Rolf Johnson, Editor , Richard Jensen; University of Nebraska Press, 2000

52   Happy as a Big Sunflower; Rolf Johnson, Editor , Richard Jensen; University of Nebraska Press, 2000

53 *Nebraska Advertiser*; January 2, 1879

54   The Walker Ranch was established by Charles Walker in 1872 as a station on the government mail (Pony Express) route from Kearney City to the Republican Valley; Source: Nebraska Historical Society

55 *Nebraska Advertiser*, January 2, 1879

56   Happy as a Big Sunflower; Rolf Johnson, Editor , Richard Jensen; University of Nebraska Press, 2000

57 *Omaha Evening News*; April 26, 1879

58   Reporters from across the Country came and were granted interviews by Richards; among them were *The Chicago Inter Ocean*; the *Nemaha Nebraska Advertiser*, *The Omaha Evening News*; *The Nebraska Republican*; and several others.

59   *Omaha Evening News*; April 26, 1879; *The Omaha Daily Republican*; April 27, 1879; & Happy as a Big Sunflower; Rolf Johnson, Editor , Richard Jensen; University of Nebraska Press, 2000

60 *Omaha Evening News*; April 26, 1879

61   Happy as a Big Sunflower; Rolf Johnson, Editor , Richard Jensen; University of Nebraska Press, 2000

62 *The Advertiser*, December 19,1878

63   Happy as a Big Sunflower; Rolf Johnson, Editor , Richard Jensen; University of Nebraska Press, 2000

64 *Omaha Evening News*; April 26, 1879

65   Heroes Without Medals: A Pioneer History of Kearney County Nebraska; Roy C. Bang; Warp Publishing; Minden, Nebraska; 1952

66 *Omaha Evening News*; April 26, 1879

67   Heroes Without Medals: A Pioneer History of Kearney County Nebraska; Roy C. Bang; Warp Publishing; Minden, Nebraska; 1952

68   *Omaha Evening News*; April 26, 1879 & Heroes Without Medals: A Pioneer History of Kearney County Nebraska; Roy C. Bang; Warp Publishing; Minden, Nebraska; 1952

69 *Omaha Evening News*; April 26, 1879

70 *Omaha Evening News*; April 26, 1879

71 *Omaha Evening News*; April 26, 1879

72 *Omaha Daily Republican*; April 27, 1879

73   Heroes Without Medals: A Pioneer History of Kearney County Nebraska; Roy C. Bang; Warp Publishing; Minden, Nebraska; 1952

74 *Omaha Evening News*; April 26, 1879

75 *The Nebraska Advertiser*, December 19, 1878

76 *The Nebraska Advertiser*, January 2, 1879

77 *Omaha Daily Republican*; April 27, 1879

78 *Omaha Evening News*; April 26, 1879

79 *Omaha Daily Republican*; April 27, 1879

80 *Omaha Evening News*; April 26, 1879

81 *Omaha Daily Republican*; April 27, 1879 & Heroes Without Medals: A Pioneer History of Kearney County Nebraska; Roy C. Bang; Warp Publishing; Minden, Nebraska; 1952

82 *Omaha Evening News*; April 26, 1879

83 *Omaha Evening News*; April 26, 1879 & Heroes Without Medals: A Pioneer History of Kearney County Nebraska; Roy C. Bang; Warp Publishing; Minden, Nebraska; 1952

84 *Omaha Evening News*; April 26, 1879

85 *Omaha Evening News*; April 26, 1879

86 *Omaha Evening News*; April 26, 1879

87 *Omaha Daily Republican*; April 27, 1879 & Nebraska Statutes 6178 (546) and 6179 (547)

88 Heroes Without Medals: A Pioneer History of Kearney County Nebraska; Roy C. Bang; Warp Publishing; Minden, Nebraska; 1952

89 *Hastings Gazette*; April 27, 1897 & Reprinted verbatim in *The Red Cloud Chief*, May 1, 1879

90 *Hastings Gazette*; April 27, 1897 & Reprinted verbatim in *The Red Cloud Chief*, May 1, 1879

91 Happy as a Big Sunflower; Rolf Johnson, Editor , Richard Jensen; University of Nebraska Press, 2000

92 *Omaha Daily Republican*; April 27, 1879

93 Happy as a Big Sunflower; Rolf Johnson, Editor , Richard Jensen; University of Nebraska Press, 2000

94 *Omaha Daily Republican*; April 27, 1879

95 Accounts take from *Omaha Herald*; April 27, 1879; *Omaha Daily Republican*; April 27, 1879; *Omaha Evening News*; April 26, 1879, and the *Hastings Gazette*; April 27, 1897

96 Accounts take from *Omaha Herald*; April 27, 1879; *Omaha Daily Republican*; April 27, 1879; *Omaha Evening News*; April 26, 1879, and the *Hastings Gazette*; April 27, 1897

97 *Omaha Herald*; April 27, 1879

98 *Omaha Daily Republican*; April 27, 1879

99 Happy as a Big Sunflower; Rolf Johnson, Editor , Richard Jensen; University of Nebraska Press, 2000

100 *Omaha Herald*; April 27, 1879

101 Cesare Lombroso was investigating this theory and reporting from 1871 to 1876; See Criminals and Their Scientists; P. Becker & E. Wetzell Eds.; Cambridge University Press; NE; 2006

102 Heroes Without Medals: A Pioneer History of Kearney County Nebraska; Roy C. Bang; Warp Publishing; Minden, Nebraska; 1952

103 Heroes Without Medals: A Pioneer History of Kearney County Nebraska; Roy C. Bang; Warp Publishing; Minden, Nebraska; 1952; *The Columbus Journal*; July 23, 1879

104 *The Nebraska Advertiser*, February 27, 1879

105 1870 United States Census

106 Last of the Great Scouts: Buffalo Bill; Zane Grey; Grosset & Dunlap; New York; 1899; p. 309

107 *The Nebraska Advertiser*, December 19, 1878

108 *The Columbus Journal*; February 5, 1879

109 *Nebraska Advertiser*, February 27, 1879

110 *The Columbus Journal*; April 23 1879 & 9 Neb. 300, 2 N.W. 710; & Omaha Daily Bee, January 4, 1888; 2 N.W. 378; & *Columbus Journal*; May 19, 1880

111 Historical Sketch of the town of Little Falls; An Address by Mrs. Adam Casler: Herkimer Present to the County Historical Society; February 14; 1903

112 *Annual Report of the Adjutant General of the State New York*; 1896

113 General History of Seward County, Nebraska; John Waterman; Beaver Crossing, Seward County, Nebr.; 1914-1920

114 *Omaha Daily Republican*; May 21, 1879

115 *Omaha Daily Republican*; May 21, 1879

116 State of Wisconsin Proceeding of the Senate ; *List of Pardons*; January 1873; p. 86

117 General History of Seward County, Nebraska; John Waterman; Beaver Crossing, Seward County, Nebr.; 1914-1920; p. 115 & also see page 47 for Waterman's explanation of *Sod Houses* and *Dug-outs*

118 General History of Seward County, Nebraska; John Waterman; Beaver Crossing, Seward County, Nebr.; 1914-1920

119 General History of Seward County, Nebraska; John Waterman; Beaver Crossing, Seward County, Nebr.; 1914-1920

120 *Omaha Evening News*; May 21, 1879

121 General History of Seward County, Nebraska; John Waterman; Beaver Crossing, Seward County, Nebr.; 1914-1920

122 *The Nebraska Advertiser*, July 25, 1878; & History of Seward County, Nebraska; W. W. Cox; State Journal Company; Lincoln, NE; 1888

123 *The Nebraska Advertiser*, July 25, 1878

124 *The Nebraska Advertiser*, July 25, 1878

125 *Omaha Daily Republican*; May 21, 1879

126 *Nebraska Reporter;* Seward; July 18,1878 & *The Nebraska Advertiser*, July 25, 1878

127 *The Nebraska Advertiser*, July 25, 1878; & History of Seward County, Nebraska; W. W. Cox; State Journal Company; Lincoln, NE; 1888

128 *Nebraska Reporter;* Seward; July 18,1878 & *The Nebraska Advertiser*, July 25, 1878

129 General History of Seward County, Nebraska; John Waterman; Beaver Crossing, Seward County, Nebr.; 1914-1920

130*Nebraska Reporter;* Seward; July 18,1878

131*Nebraska Reporter;* Seward; July 18,1878

132Records of the Clerk of the District Court, Seward, Nebraska

133*Omaha Daily Republican;* May 21, 1879

134 General History of Seward County, Nebraska; John Waterman; Beaver Crossing, Seward County, Nebr.; 1914-1920

135*Omaha Daily Republican;* May 21, 1879

136 *Omaha Daily Republican;* May 21, 1879; & Records of the Clerk of the District Court, Seward, Nebraska

137 *The Nebraska Advertiser;* February 27, 1879;& Records of the Clerk of the District Court, Seward, Nebraska

138*Omaha Daily Republican;* May 21, 1879

139*Omaha Daily Republican;* May 21, 1879

140 General History of Seward County, Nebraska; John Waterman; Beaver Crossing, Seward County, Nebr.; 1914-1920

141 *Abstract of Census Returns for 1872;* as Reported in *The Red Cloud Chief;* July 25, 1878

142 *Population of Incorporated Places;* as Reported in the 1922 Nebraska Blue Book; Nebraska Legislature; 1922

143*Omaha Daily Republican;* May 21, 1879

144 *The Omaha Daily Herald;* May 21, 1879 placed the crowd at 5,000 & *The Omaha Evening News;* May 21, 1879 reported that the crowd was near 8,000

145*Omaha Daily Republican;* May 21, 1879

146*The Omaha Daily Herald;* May 21, 1879

147*The Omaha Daily Herald;* May 21, 1879

148*Omaha Daily Republican;* May 21, 1879

149 General History of Seward County, Nebraska; John Waterman; Beaver Crossing, Seward County, Nebr.; 1914-1920

150*Omaha Daily Republican;* May 21, 1879

151*The Omaha Daily Herald;* May 21, 1879

152Records of the Clerk of the District Court, Seward, Nebraska

153Nebraska State Historical Society

154*Osceola Reporter;* March 13, 1885

155*Omaha Daily Bee;* July 25, 1885

156Records of the *United States Census 1850*

157Records of the *United States Census, 1850*

158 Osceola 1871 – 1971; Osceola Centennial Book Committee; Union College Press, Lincoln, NE; 1972 & Records of the *United States Census*

159 Osceola 1871 – 1971; Osceola Centennial Book Committee; Union College Press, Lincoln, NE; 1972

160 Osceola 1871 – 1971; Osceola Centennial Book Committee; Union College Press, Lincoln, NE; 1972 & Omaha Daily Republican; July 25, 1885

161 Osceola 1871 – 1971; Osceola Centennial Book Committee; Union College Press, Lincoln, NE; 1972 & Omaha Daily Republican; July 25, 1885

162 *Records of the Clerk of the District Court's Office; Polk County; Divorce Petition of Ruth Smith; July 15; 1884*

163 *The Nebraska Advertiser; March 30, 1876*

164 *The Columbus Journal*; December 3, 1884

165 Records of the Clerk of the District Court's Office; Polk County; Divorce Petition of Ruth Smith; July 15; 1884

166 *The Daily Nebraska State Journal*; Saturday, July 25, 1885

167 *The Daily Nebraska State Journal*; Saturday, July 25, 1885

168 Records of the Clerk of the District Court's Office; Polk County; Divorce Petition of Ruth Smith; July 15; 1884

169 Osceola 1871 – 1971; Osceola Centennial Book Committee; Union College Press, Lincoln, NE; 1972

170 Osceola 1871 – 1971; Osceola Centennial Book Committee; Union College Press, Lincoln, NE; 1972

171 *The Daily Nebraska State Journal*; Saturday, July 25, 1885

172 Osceola 1871 – 1971; Osceola Centennial Book Committee; Union College Press, Lincoln, NE; 1972 & Records of the Clerk of the District Court's Office; Polk County; Divorce Petition of Ruth Smith; July 15; 1884

173 *Omaha Daily Republican*; July 25, 1885

174 Osceola 1871 – 1971; Osceola Centennial Book Committee; Union College Press, Lincoln, NE; 1972

175 *Omaha Daily Republican*; July 25, 1885 & *The Daily Nebraska State Journal*; Saturday, July 25, 1885

176 Osceola 1871 – 1971; Osceola Centennial Book Committee; Union College Press, Lincoln, NE; 1972

177 *The Daily Nebraska State Journal*; Saturday, July 25, 1885

178 *Omaha Daily Bee*; July 25, 1885 & *Omaha Daily Republican*; July 25, 1885 & *The Daily Nebraska State Journal*; Saturday, July 25, 1885

179 Records of the Clerk of the District Court's Office; Polk County; Indictment of Milton W. Smith

180 Records of the Clerk of the District Court's Office; Polk County; Coroner's Arrest Warrant for Milton Smith

181 *The Omaha Daily Bee*; December 22, 1884

182 Records of the Clerk of the District Court's Office; Polk County; Grand Jury Indictment

183 *Omaha Daily Bee*; July 25, 1885 & *The Daily Nebraska State Journal*; Saturday, July 25, 1885 & Records of the Clerk of the District Court's Office

184 Records of the Clerk of the District Court's Office; Polk County & Osceola 1871 – 1971; Osceola Centennial Book Committee; Union College Press, Lincoln, NE; 1972

185 <u>Osceola 1871 – 1971</u>; Osceola Centennial Book Committee; Union College Press, Lincoln, NE; 1972 & *The Daily Nebraska State Journal*; Saturday, July 25, 1885

186 *The Daily Nebraska State Journal*; Saturday, July 25, 1885 & Records of the Clerk of the District Court's Office; Polk County; Jury and Witness Lists

187 Records of the Clerk of the District Court's Office; Polk County; Witness Subpoenas & *The Daily Nebraska State Journal*; Saturday, July 25, 1885

188 *The Daily Nebraska State Journal*; Saturday, July 25, 1885

189 Records of the Clerk of the District Court's Office; Polk County; Verdict of Jury; & *Osceola Record*; March 26; 1885

190 *Osceola Record*; March 26; 1885; & *Osceola Record*; March 26; 1885 & Records of the Clerk of the District Court's Office; Polk County; Verdict of Jury

191 Records of the Clerk of the District Court's Office; Polk County; Appeal for a New Trial; & *Omaha Daily Bee*; July 25, 1885

192 *Osceola Record*; March 26

193 *The Daily Nebraska State Journal*; Saturday, July 25, 1885

194 *The Omaha Daily Bee*; July 24, 1885

195 *The Omaha Daily Bee*; July 24, 1885

196 <u>Osceola 1871 – 1971</u>; Osceola Centennial Book Committee; Union College Press, Lincoln, NE; 1972

197 *The Daily Nebraska State Journal*; Saturday, July 25, 1885 & <u>Osceola 1871 – 1971</u>; Osceola Centennial Book Committee; Union College Press, Lincoln, NE; 1972

198 *The Daily Nebraska State Journal*; Saturday, July 25, 1885

199 *The Omaha Daily Bee*; July 25, 1885

200 The *Omaha Daily Bee*; July 25, 1885

201 The *Omaha Daily Bee*; July 25, 1885

202 *The Daily Nebraska State Journal*; Saturday, July 25, 1885

203 The *Omaha Daily Bee*; October 11, 1891

204 The Account of the Hanging taken from; *The Daily Nebraska State Journal*; Saturday, July 25, 1885; & The *Omaha Daily Bee*; July 25, 1885 & Omaha Daily Republican; July 25, 1885

205 *The Daily Nebraska State Journal*; Saturday, July 25, 1885

206 The Account of the Hanging taken from; *The Daily Nebraska State Journal*; Saturday, July 25, 1885; & The *Omaha Daily Bee*; July 25, 1885 & Omaha Daily Republican; July 25, 1885

207 *Omaha Daily Bee*; July 25, 1885

208 *The Omaha Daily Republican*; July 25, 1885 & files.usgwarchives.net/ne/polk/cemeteries/cem06.txt

209 <u>History of Western Nebraska and Its People: Volume II</u>; Grant Shumway; Western Publishing and Engraving; Lincoln, NE; 1921; p. 166

210 *Washington Evening Star*; July 9, 1876; *Dodge City Times*; October 12, 1878

211 History of Western Nebraska and Its People: Volume II; Grant Shumway; Western Publishing and Engraving; Lincoln, NE; 1921; p. 166

212 Historical Dictionary of the Gilded Age

213 The Pole Creek Crossing; Loren Avey; Author House, Bloomington, Indiana; 2010

214 History of Western Nebraska and Its People: Volume II; Grant Shumway; Western Publishing and Engraving; Lincoln, NE; 1921; p. 171

215 *The Omaha Daily Bee*; January 16, 1877

216 Letter of Jesse James purportedly planning the Big Springs Robbery; Life and Adventures of Frank and Jesse James; J. A. Dacus; W. S. Brfan; San Francisco; 1880; p. 339

217 History of Western Nebraska and Its People: Volume II; Grant Shumway; Western Publishing and Engraving; Lincoln, NE; 1921; p. 175

218 *The Omaha Daily Bee*; May 22. 1886

219 *The Omaha Daily Bee*; May 22. 1886 & Lynchings, Legends, and Lawlessness; Loren Avey; City of Sidney & Hughes Designs LLC; 2004

220 *The Omaha Daily Bee*; September 18, 1885

221 *The McCook Tribune*; May 27, 1886

222 *The McCook Tribune*; May 27, 1886 & *The McCook Tribune*; September 24, 1885

223 *The McCook Tribune*; May 27, 1886

224 *The Omaha Daily Bee*; September 18, 1885 & *The Nebraska State Journal*; September 19, 1885

225 *The McCook Tribune*; May 27, 1886

226 *The McCook Tribune*; September 24, 1885

227 *The Omaha Daily Bee*; September 18, 1885

228 *The McCook Tribune*; September 24, 1885

229 Records of the Cheyenne County District Court

230 *The McCook Tribune*; May 27, 1886 & *Nebraska History*; Potter; Vol. 93; Issue ; 2012; p. 139

231 *The Omaha Daily Bee*; May 20, 1886

232 *The McCook Tribune*; May 27, 1886

233 *The McCook Tribune*; May 27, 1886

234 *The Omaha Daily Bee*; May 22, 1886

235 *The Omaha Daily Herald*; May 22, 1886

236 *The McCook Tribune*; May 27, 1886

237 *The Omaha Daily Bee*; May 22, 1886

238 *The Omaha Daily Bee*; May 18, 1886

239 *The Omaha Daily Bee*; May 20, 1886

240 *The Omaha Daily Bee*; May 22, 1886

241 *The McCook Tribune*; May 27, 1886

242 *The McCook Tribune*; May 27, 1886

243 *The McCook Tribune*; May 27, 1886

244 *The Omaha Daily Bee*; May 22, 1886

245 *The Daily Nebraska State Journal*, Saturday, September 19, 1885

246 *The Daily Nebraska State Journal*, Saturday, September 19, 1885 & *The Omaha Daily Bee*; May 22, 1886

247 *The Omaha Herald*; May 22, 1886

248 *The Daily Nebraska State Journal*, Saturday, September 19, 1885 & *The Daily Nebraska State Journal*, Saturday, September 19, 1885 & Lynchings, Legends, and Lawlessness; Loren Avey; City of Sidney & Hughes Designs LLC; 2004

249 Lynchings, Legends, and Lawlessness; Loren Avey; City of Sidney & Hughes Designs LLC; 2004

250 North Platte Semi-Weekly Tribune; September 1, 1922

251 Records of Fort McPherson National Cemetery

252 Annual Report of the Commissioner of Indian Affairs; Government Printing Office; Washington, D.C.; 1880

253 *The Nebraska Advertiser*; February 25, 1869 & *The Nebraska Advertiser*; February 3, 1870

254 Encyclopedia of the Great Plains; Published as a project of the Center for Great Plains Studies edited by David Wishart; 2004; p. 588

255 *Nebraska Historic Buildings Survey Reconnaissance Survey: Final Report of Gage County, Nebraska*; Dr. Kathleen Fimple; Nebraska State Historical Society; August 1, 1992

256 Annual Report of the Board of the Railroad Commission for the year 1883; Published by the Kansas Board of Railroad Commissioners; T. D. Thatcher; Official Kansas Printer; 1884 & *Asher-Adams RR Map of 1873*; Historic Map Collection, Omaha Public Library; Omaha, NE

257 *Beatrice Weekly Express*; March 27, 1873

258 Witness Testimony; Cited from 20 Neb. 233, 29 N.W. 911 (Note: Original Records of the Gage District Court were either lost or stolen)

259 Rachel Warren's testimony, repeated verbatim in the Nebraska Supreme Court Record; 20 Neb. 233, 29 N.W. 911

260 *Beatrice Weekly Express*; March 27, 1873

261 *Beatrice Weekly Express*; March 20, 1873

262 *Beatrice Weekly Express*; March 27, 1873

263 *Beatrice Weekly Express*; March 27, 1873

264 *Beatrice Weekly Express*; March 27, 1873

265 *Beatrice Weekly Express*; March 27, 1873

266 *Beatrice Weekly Express*; April 10, 1873

267 *Omaha Daily Herald*; March 25; 1887

268 A History of the State of Oklahoma; Luther B. Hill; Lewis Publishing; New York; 1910; p. 386

269 *The Omaha Daily Bee*; March 26, 1887

270 *Beatrice Weekly Express*; January 5, 1883

271 16 Neb. 349

272 *Beatrice Weekly Express*; May 4, 1883

273 20 Neb. 233, 29 N.W. 911

274 *Gage County Democrat*; May 6, 1883

275 *Beatrice Weekly Express*; May 4, 1883

276 *The Omaha Daily Bee*; March 26, 1887 & *Beatrice Weekly Express*; May 4, 1883

277 *The Omaha Daily Bee*; March 26, 1887 & *Gage County Democrat*; May 4, 1883

278 16 Neb. 349, 20 N.W. 289

279 *Gage County Democrat*; March 6, 1885

280 *Gage County Democrat*; March 13, 1885

281 *Omaha Daily Herald*; March 25; 1887 & *The Omaha Daily Bee*; June 17, 1885

282 20 Neb. 233, 29 N.W. 911

283 *Gage County Democrat*; March 31, 1887 & 20 Neb. 233, 29 N.W. 911

284 History of Gage County Nebraska; Hugh Dobbs; Western Publishing, Lincoln, NE; 1918; p. 199

285 *Nebraska Advertiser*; June 11, 1874

286 The Omaha Daily Bee; June 16, 1874

287 Interview with Lesa Arterburn; Executive Director; Gage County Historical Society

288 Census printed in *The Red Cloud Chief*; November 30, 1900 & *Gage County Democrat*; February 10, 1887 & *Gage County Democrat*; March 31, 1887

289 Bad Men and Bad Towns; Wayne C. Lee; Caxton Press, Caldwell, ID; 2010; p. 80

290 *Omaha Daily Bee*; March 23, 1887

291 *Gage County Democrat*; March 24, 1887 & *Gage County Democrat*; March 26, 1887

292 *Gage County Democrat*; March 24, 1887

293 *Gage County Democrat*; March 31, 1887 & *Gage County Democrat*; March 24, 1887

294 *The McCook Tribune*; March 31, 1887

295 The Description of Marion's hanging is a compilation of reports from: *Daily Nebraska State Journal*; March 26, 1887 & *Omaha Daily Bee*; March 26, 1887; & *Gage County Democrat*; March 31, 1887

296 The Description of Marion's hanging is a compilation of reports from: *Daily Nebraska State Journal*; March 26, 1887 & *Omaha Daily Bee*; March 26,

1887; & *Gage County Democrat*; March 31, 1887

297 *Omaha World Herald*; March 25, 1887

298 *Gage County Democrat*; March 31, 1887

299 *Morning World Herald*; Tuesday, August 4, 1891 & *The Beatrice Daily Express:* August 3, 1891

300 *Morning World Herald*; Tuesday, August 4, 1891 & *The Beatrice Daily Express:* August 3, 1891

301 *The Beatrice Daily Express:* August 3, 1891 & *Omaha Daily Bee*; August 4, 1891

302 Omaha Daily Bee; March 26, 1887

303 Records of the Nebraska Secretary of State's Office

304 The Official History of The Great Strike of 1886; Bureau of Labor Statistics and Inspection of Missouri; Tribune Printing; Jefferson City, MO; 1886

305 The Official History of The Great Strike of 1886; Bureau of Labor Statistics and Inspection of Missouri; Tribune Printing; Jefferson City, MO; 1886; p. 116

306 *Iola Register*; April 30, 1886

307 *The Emporia Weekly News*; September 15, 1877

308 The Official History of The Great Strike of 1886; Bureau of Labor Statistics and Inspection of Missouri; Tribune Printing; Jefferson City, MO; 1886 & The Emporia Weekly

309 *Daily Nebraska Press*; January 12, 1887 & *Nebraska City News Press*; April 10, 1983

310 *The Omaha Daily Bee*; January 13, 1887

311 *Omaha Daily World*; January 12, 1887

312 *The Omaha Daily Bee*; January 13, 1887

313 *Daily Nebraska Press*; January 13, 1887 & *Omaha Daily Bee*; January 13, 1887

314 *The Omaha Daily Bee*; July 22, 1887

315 *Daily Nebraska Press*; January 13, 1887 & *Omaha Daily Bee*; June 16, 1880 & *Pettigill's Newspaper Directory*; 1903; p. 362

316 *Omaha Daily World*; April 7, 1887

317 *Iola Register*: January 21, 1887 & *Omaha Dailey Bee*; April 8, 1887

318 *The Omaha Daily World*; April 7, 1887

319 *The Omaha Dailey Bee*; April 7, 1887

320 *The Omaha Dailey Bee*; April 9, 1887

321 *The Omaha Dailey Bee*; April 9, 1887

322 *Omaha Daily World*; July 22, 1887 & *Omaha Dailey Bee*; April 9, 1887 & *Omaha Dailey Bee*; July 22, 1887

323 *Omaha Dailey Bee*; April 9, 1887 & *Omaha Dailey Bee*; July 22, 1887

324 *The Omaha Republican*; April 12, 1887 & the Records of the Nebraska Department of Corrections

325 *The Omaha Republican*; July 23 1887 & *The Omaha Dailey Bee*; July 22, 1887

326 The McCook Tribune; January 17, 1887

327 *The Omaha Dailey Bee*; July 22, 1887

328 *The Omaha Dailey Bee*; July 22, 1887

329 *The Omaha Republican*; July 23 1887

330 *Daily Nebraska Press*; July 23, 1887 & *The Omaha Republican*; July 23 1887

331 The account of Hoffman's hanging taken from: *The Omaha Republican*; July 23 1887; *The Omaha Dailey Bee*; July 22, 1887; and *Omaha Daily Herald*; July 22, 1887

332 *The Omaha Republican*; July 23 1887 & *The Omaha Dailey Bee*; July 22, 1887

333 *The Omaha Republican*; July 23 1887 & *The Omaha Dailey Bee*; July 22, 1887

334 *The Omaha Dailey Bee*; July 22, 1887

335 Records of the Nebraska Department of Corrections

336 Nebraska State Historical Society

337 Empire on the Platte; Richard Crabb; The World Publishing C.; Cleveland & New York; 1967

338 *The Omaha Daily Bee;* November 13, 1888 & The *Evening World Herald*; May 22, 1891

339 Steven J Ramold, "'Altogether a Horrible Spectacle': Public Executions in Nebraska, 1891," *Nebraska History* 86 (2005): 62-77

340 *The Omaha Daily Bee*; July 22, 1891

341 Pioneer History of Custer County; Solomon Bucher & E. Finch; Merchants Publishing, Denver; 1901

342 *The Omaha Daily Bee*, November 26, 1888

343 *The Omaha Daily Bee*, November 26, 1888 & *The McCook Tribune*; December 7, 1888

344 *The McCook Tribune*; December 7, 1888

345 *The Omaha Daily Bee*, November 13, 1888

346 *The Omaha Daily Bee*, November 21, 1888

347 *The Columbus Journal*; November 28, 1888

348   *The Columbus Journal*; November 28, 1888 & *The Omaha Daily Bee*, November 26, 1888

349 *The McCook Tribune*; December 7, 1888

350 Neb. 112, 47 N.W. 698

351 History of Custer County Nebraska; W. Gaston & A. Humphrey; Western Publishing, Lincoln; 1919

352 Steven J Ramold, "'Altogether a Horrible Spectacle': Public Executions in Nebraska, 1891," *Nebraska History* 86 (2005): 62-77 & *Columbus Journal*;

September 11, 1889

353 Neb. 112, 47 N.W. 698 & *Columbus Journal*; January 7, 1891

354 *Omaha Daily Herald*; April 18, 1891

355 *The Omaha Daily Bee*; April 18, 1891 & May 22, 1891 & the *Omaha Daily Herald*; April 18, 1891

356 *Omaha Daily Herald*; April 18, 1891 & *The Omaha Daily Bee;* April 18, 1891 & *The Columbus Journal*; April 22, 1891

357 *The Omaha Daily Bee;* May 22, 1891

358 *The Omaha Daily Bee;* May 22, 1891

359 *The Omaha Daily Bee;* May 22, 1891 & <u>Pioneer History of Custer County</u>; Solomon Bucher & E. Finch; Merchants Publishing, Denver; 1901

360 *The Omaha Daily Bee;* May 22, 1891 & *The Omaha Daily Bee;* May 23, 1891

361 *The Omaha Daily Bee;* May 22, 1891

362 *Evening World- Herald*; May 22, 1891

363 *The Omaha Daily Bee;* May 23, 1891 & the *Morning World Herald*; May 23, 1891

364 *The Omaha Daily Bee;* May 23, 1891 & the *Morning World Herald*; May 23, 1891

365 *Moming World- Herald*; May 23, 1891

366 *The Omaha Daily Bee;* May 23, 1891

367 <u>History of Dodge and Washington Counties, Nebraska and Their People</u>; William Buss & Thomas Osterman, Editors; The American Historical Society; Chicago; 1921 & "Now" in Parenthesis referred to was 1921

368 <u>History of Dodge and Washington Counties, Nebraska and Their People</u>; William Buss & Thomas Osterman, Editors; The American Historical Society; Chicago; 1921

369 *The Omaha Daily Bee*, December 12, 1889

370 Civil War Record of the National Park Service on Line

371 *The Omaha Daily Bee*, December 11, 1889

372 *Fremont Weekly Herald*; June 6, 1891

373 31 Neb. 389, 47 N.W. 1118

374 *Fremont Weekly Herald*; June 6, 1891 & *The Omaha Daily Bee*, December 12, 1889 & 31 Neb. 389, 47 N.W. 1118

375 *The Omaha Daily Bee*, December 12, 1889 & *Fremont Weekly Herald*; June 6, 1891

376 31 Neb. 389, 47 N.W. 1118 & *The Omaha Daily Bee*, December 12, 1889

377 *The Omaha Daily Bee*; March 21, 1890

378 *The Omaha Daily Bee*; December 12, 1889 & *The Omaha Daily Bee*; January 30, 1890

379 *The Omaha Daily Bee*; December 13, 1889 & *Fremont Weekly Herald*; June 6, 1891

380 31 Neb. 389, 47 N.W. 1118 & *The Omaha Daily Bee*, December 13, 1889

381 *The Omaha Daily Bee*, December 13, 1889

382 *The Omaha Daily Bee*; February 2, 1890 & *The Omaha Daily Bee*; March 23, 1890

383 Records of the Clerk of the District Court; Dodge County Nebraska

384 Records of the Clerk of the District Court; Dodge County Nebraska

385 Records of the Dodge County District Court; Herman Diers v. James P. Mallon & Frank Pulsifer

386 *Lincoln County Tribune*; December 25, 1889 & Herman Diers v. James P. Mallon & Frank Pulsifer

387 *The Omaha Daily Bee*; January 28, 1890 & *The Omaha Daily Bee*; January 30, 1890

388 *The Omaha Daily Bee*; February 1, 1890 & *Fremont Weekly Herald*; February 6, 1890

389 *Fremont Weekly Herald*; February 6, 1890

390 *The Omaha Daily Bee*; February 2, 1890 & Steven J Ramold, "'Altogether a Horrible Spectacle': Public Executions in Nebraska, 1891," *Nebraska History* 86 (2005): 62-77

391 *The Omaha Daily Bee*; February 2, 1890

392 *The Red Cloud Chief*; March 14, 1890

393 *The Omaha Daily Bee*; March 18, 19, & 20, 1890

394 *The Omaha Daily Bee*; March 20, 21, & 23, 1890

395 *The Omaha Daily Bee*; March 23, 1890

396 *The Omaha Daily Bee*; March 23, 1890

397 Records of the Dodge County Clerk of the District Court; Jury Verdict; State v. Furst

398 *The Omaha Daily Bee*; March 26, 1890

399 *The Omaha Daily Bee*; April 15, 1890

400 31 Neb. 389, 47 N.W. 1118 & 31 Neb. 403, 47 N.W. 1116

401 31 Neb. 389, 47 N.W. 1118

402 31 Neb. 403, 47 N.W. 1116

403 Records of the Dodge County Nebraska Clerk of the District Court; Death Warrants for Shepard and Furst

404 *The Omaha Daily Bee*; April 25, 1891

405 *The McCook Tribune*; May 15, 1891

406 *The Omaha Daily Bee;* May 23, 1891 & the *Morning World Herald*; May 23, 1891 & *Fremont Weekly Herald*; June 6, 1891

407 *Fremont Weekly Herald*; June 6, 1891

408 *Nebraska Memories*; Nebraska Library Commission; Dodge County Jail; http://memories.ne.gov/

409 Statutes of Nebraska, 1891; J. E. Cobbey, Esq., of the Beatrice Bar; State Journal Company, Lincoln; p. 1222

410 *Fremont Weekly Herald*; June 6, 1891

411 *Evening World Herald*; June 5, 1891 & *Fremont Weekly Herald*; June 6, 1891 & 143 U.S. 135, 12 S. Ct. 375

412 *Fremont Weekly Herald*; June 6, 1891

413 *Fremont Weekly Herald*; June 6, 1891

414 Account of the hanging from: *Fremont Weekly Herald*; June 6, 1891 & *The Omaha Daily Bee*, June 6, 1891

415 Account of the hanging from: *Fremont Weekly Herald*; June 6, 1891 & *The Omaha Daily Bee*, June 6, 1891

416 *The Omaha Daily Bee*, June 6, 1891

417 Records of the Clerk of the District Court of Dodge County

418 *The Omaha Daily Bee*; October 10, 1891

419 Nebraska Supreme Court; Neal v. State, 32 Neb. 120, 49 N.W. 174, June 29, 1891

420 *The Omaha Daily Bee*; October 10, 1891 and *History at a Glance*; Douglas County Historical Society; Author Liz Rea, Director of Education; p. 69

421 Nebraska Supreme Court; Neal v. State, 32 Neb. 120, 49 N.W. 174, June 29, 1891 & *Omaha Daily World Herald*; February 14, 1890

422 Nebraska Supreme Court; Neal v. State, 32 Neb. 120, 49 N.W. 174, June 29, 1891

423 *Omaha Daily World-Herald*; February 14, 1890

424 Nebraska Supreme Court; Neal v. State, 32 Neb. 120, 49 N.W. 174, June 29, 1891 and *The Omaha Daily Bee*; October 10, 1891

425 *The Omaha Daily Bee*; October 10, 1891

426 Nebraska Supreme Court; Neal v. State, 32 Neb. 120, 49 N.W. 174, June 29, 1891 & *Omaha Daily World Herald*; February 14, 1890

427 *Omaha Daily World-Herald*; February 14, 1890 & Neal v. State, 32 Neb. 120, 49 N.W. 174, June 29, 1891

428 *Omaha Daily World-Herald*; February 14, 1890

429 *Omaha Daily World-Herald*; February 14, 1890

430 Nebraska Supreme Court; Neal v. State, 32 Neb. 120, 49 N.W. 174, June 29, 1891

431 *Omaha Daily World- Herald*; February 15, 1890

432 Neal v. State, 32 Neb. 120, 49 N.W. 174

433 Nebraska Supreme Court; Neal v. State, 32 Neb. 120, 49 N.W. 174, June 29, 1891

434 *The Omaha Daily Bee*; October 10, 1891

435 *The Omaha Daily Bee*; October 10, 1891

436 *The Omaha Daily Bee*; October 10, 1891

437 *Omaha Daily World-Herald*; March 2, 1890

438 *Omaha Daily World-Herald*; March 2, 1890

439 *Omaha Daily World-Herald*; March 2, 1890

440 *The Omaha-World-Herald*; May 13, 1890

441 *The Omaha Republican*; May 16, 1890

442 *The Omaha Republican*; May 18, 1890

443 *The Omaha Republican*; May 20, 1890

444 *The Omaha Republican*; May 22, 1890

445 *The Omaha Daily Bee*; July 13, 1890 & *The Omaha Republican*; May 22, 1890

446 *The Omaha Daily Bee*; July 13, 1890

447 Nebraska Supreme Court; Neal v. State, 32 Neb. 120, 49 N.W. 174, June 29, 1891

448 *The Omaha Daily Bee*; October 10, 1891

449 *Morning World-Herald*, October 9, 1891

450 *Morning World-Herald*, October 10, 1891

451 *The Omaha Daily Bee*; October 10, 1891

452 *Morning World Herald*, October 10, 1891 and *Omaha Daily Bee*; October 10, 1891

453 *Morning World-Herald*, October 10, 1891

454 *Morning World-Herald*; October 13, 1891

455 Morning Edition of the *Omaha Daily Bee*, October 9, 1891

456 Records of the Catholic Cemeteries of the Archdiocese of Omaha

457 *The McCook Tribune*; August 5, 1892

458 *The Omaha Daily Bee*; November 14, 1892

459 *The Ontario Argus*; November 14, 1892

460 *The Omaha Daily Bee*; August 7, 1909

461 *The Omaha Daily Bee*; August 11, 1909

462 Thomas R Buecker, "Fort Niobrara, 1880-1906: Guardian of the Rosebud Sioux," Nebraska History 65: (1984): 301-325

463 Records of the *Nebraska State Historical Society*

464 Records of the *Nebraska State Historical Society*

465 Thomas R Buecker, "Fort Niobrara, 1880-1906: Guardian of the Rosebud Sioux," Nebraska History 65: (1984): 301-325

466 Thomas R Buecker, "Fort Niobrara, 1880-1906: Guardian of the Rosebud Sioux," Nebraska History 65: (1984): 301-325

467 *Omaha Daily World*, June 16, 1888

468 Records of the Cherry County Clerk of the District Court's Office

469 *The Omaha Daily Bee*; November 26, 1891

470 *The Omaha Daily Bee*; December 15, 1891

471 *The Omaha Daily Bee*; June 24, 1892

472 *The Evening World-Herald*, June 24, 1892

473 *The Omaha Daily Bee*; December 15, 1891

474 *The Evening World-Herald*, June 24, 1892

475 *The Evening World-Herald*, June 24, 1892

476 *The Evening World-Herald*, June 24, 1892

477   Records of the trial transcripts U. S. v Dixon; U. S. Circuit Court, National Archives, Kansas City, Missouri

478 *The Omaha Daily Bee*; December 15, 1891

479 *The Evening World-Herald*, June 24, 1892

480   Records of the trial transcripts U. S. v Dixon; U. S. Circuit Court, National Archives, Kansas City, Missouri

481   Grave located at www.findagrave.com/Fort Niobrara Post Cemetery; No birth date; died Oct. 1, 1891

482 *The Omaha Daily Bee*; November 26, 1891

483   Records of the trial transcripts U. S. v Dixon; U. S. Circuit Court, National Archives, Kansas City, Missouri

484   United States ex rel. Standing Bear v. Crook; 5 Dill. 453, 25 F.Cas. 695

485   Records of the trial transcripts U. S. v Dixon; U. S. Circuit Court, National Archives, Kansas City, Missouri

486 *The Omaha Daily Bee*; December 15, 1891

487   Records of the trial transcripts U. S. v Dixon; U. S. Circuit Court, National Archives, Kansas City, Missouri

488 *The Omaha Daily Bee*; December 15, 1891

489   Records of the trial transcripts U. S. v Dixon; U. S. Circuit Court, National Archives, Kansas City, Missouri

490   *The Omaha Daily Bee*; December 17, 1891 and U. S. v Dixon; U. S. Circuit Court

491 *The Omaha Daily Bee*; December 17, 1891

492   Records of the trial transcripts U. S. v Dixon; U. S. Circuit Court, National Archives, Kansas City, Missouri

493 *The Omaha Daily Bee*; December 17, 1891

494   Records of the trial transcripts U. S. v Dixon; U. S. Circuit Court, National Archives, Kansas City, Missouri

495 *The Omaha Daily Bee*; January 8, 1992

496   Records of the trial transcripts U. S. v Dixon; U. S. Circuit Court, National Archives, Kansas City, Missouri

497 *The Evening World-Herald*, March 11, 1892

498 *The Evening World-Herald*, March 11, 1892

499 *The Evening World-Herald*, March 14, 1892

500 *The Evening World-Herald*, April 6, 1892

501   *The Evening World-Herald*, April 16, 1892 and *The Evening World Herald*, April 18, 1892

502 *The Evening World-Herald*, April 16, 1892

503 *The Evening World-Herald*, April 18, 1892

504 *The Evening World-Herald*, April 19, 1892

505 *The Omaha Daily Bee*; October 16, 1891

506 *The Evening World Herald*, May 6, 1892

507 *The Evening World Herald*, May 16, 1892

508 Records of the trial transcripts U. S. v Dixon; U. S. Circuit Court, National Archives, Kansas City, Missouri

509 *The Evening World Herald*, June 21, 1892 and *The Evening World Herald*, June 22, 1892

510 *The Omaha Daily Bee*; June 24, 1892

511 *The Evening World-Herald*, June 24, 1892

512 *The Omaha Daily Bee*; June 25, 1892

513 *The Evening World-Herald*, June 24, 1892

514 *The Evening World-Herald*, June 24, 1892

515 *The Omaha Daily Bee*; June 25, 1892

516 *The Omaha Daily Bee*; June 25, 1892

517 *The Evening World-Herald*, June 25, 1892

518 *The Evening World-Herald*, June 25, 1892

519 History of Cass County, Nebraska; *The Plattsmouth Journal*; Project Coordinator, Mary Skalak; Curtis Media Corporation; 1989

520 The Portrait and Biographical Album of Otoe and Cass Counties, Nebraska; Chapman Brothers; Chicago; 1889

521 The Portrait and Biographical Album of Otoe and Cass Counties, Nebraska; Chapman Brothers; Chicago; 1889

522 *Evening World Herald*; December 21, 1893

523 *The Omaha Daily Bee*; November 2, 1893 & *Evening World Herald*; December 15, 1893

524 *The Omaha Daily Bee*; December 12, 1893

525 *The Omaha Daily Bee*; November 2, 1893 & *Evening World Herald*; December 15 & 21, 1893

526 *Morning World-Herald*; November 3, 1893

527 *The Omaha Daily Bee*; November 4, 1893

528 *The Omaha Daily Bee*; November 4, 1893

529 *The Omaha Daily Bee*; November 4, 1893 & *The Omaha Daily Bee*; December 12, 1893

530 *The Omaha Daily Bee*; November 5, 1893

531 *The Omaha Daily Bee*; November 5, 1893

532 *Omaha World Herald*; November 5, 1893

533 Records of the Cass County Clerk of the District Court & *The Omaha Daily Bee*; December 12, 1893

534 *The Omaha Daily Bee*; December 12, 1893

535 *The Omaha Daily Bee*; December 13, 1893

536 *Evening World Herald*; December 14, 1893 & *The Omaha Daily Bee*; December 13 & 14, 1893

537 *The Omaha Daily Bee*; December 16, 1893

538 *The Omaha Daily Bee*; December 16, 1893

539 *The Morning World Herald;* December 18, 1893 & *Omaha Daily Bee*; December 18, 1893

540 *The Morning World Herald;* December 19, 1893 & *Omaha Daily Bee*; December 19, 1893

541 *Omaha Daily Bee*; December 20, 1893 & The *Evening World Herald*; December 20, 1893

542 *Evening World Herald;* December 21, 1893 & *Omaha Daily Bee*; December 21, 1893

543 *Evening World Herald;* December 21, 1893

544 *Sunday World Herald*; December 24, 1893

545 *The Omaha Daily Bee*; December 27, 1893

546 *The Omaha Daily Bee*; December 27, 1893

547 *Evening World Herald;* December 21, 1893

548 *Evening World Herald*; January 28, 1894

549 Harlen Seyfer; Plattsmouth Public Library; *Between the Pages*; The Ladies and the Murderer; November 2012

550 Joseph R. Gusfield; Social Structure and Moral Reform: A Study of the Woman's Christian Temperance Union; *American Journal of Sociology*, Vol. 61, No. 3 (Nov., 1955), pp. 221

551 *The Omaha Daily Bee*; March 21, 1894

55242 Neb. 503, 60 N.W. 916

553 Records of the Cass County Clerk of the District Court

554 *The Omaha Daily Bee*; February 5, 1895

555 *The Omaha Daily Bee*; February 23 & 25, 1895

556 *The Omaha Daily Bee*; March 1, 1895

557 *Evening World-Herald*; March 1, 1895 & *The Omaha Daily Bee*; March 2, 1895

558 *Evening World-Herald*; March 1, 1895 & *The Omaha Daily Bee*; March 2, 1895

559 *The Omaha Daily Bee*; March 2, 1895

560 *The Omaha Daily Bee*; July 20, 1899

561 *The Omaha Daily Bee*; October 18, 1890

562 Personal Author Interviews; Summer 2013

563 An Essay on Crimes and Punishments; Cesare Beccaria; Translated by Monf. De Voltaire; Printed by Newberry; London; 1775

564 *The Omaha Daily Bee*; December 30, 1895

565 *The Evening World-Herald*, December 14, 1895

566 *The Omaha Daily Bee*; December 28, 1895 and *The Omaha Daily Bee*; October 13, 1895

567 *The Omaha Daily Bee*; November 2, 1895

568 *The Omaha Daily Bee*; November 4, 1895

569 *The Omaha Daily Bee*; December 28, 1895

570 *The Evening World-Herald*, December 14, 1895

571 *The Omaha Daily Bee*; December 28, 1895

572 Hoover v. State; 48 Neb. 184, 66 N. W. 1117

573 *The Omaha Daily Bee*; December 28, 1895

574 *The Omaha Daily Bee*; December 28, 1895 and Hoover v. State; 48 Neb. 184, 66 N. W. 1117

575 *The Omaha Daily Bee*; December 14, 1895 and *The Omaha Daily Bee*; December 28, 1895

576 *The Evening World Herald*, December 14, 1895

577 *The Omaha Daily Bee*; December 28, 1895

578 *The Omaha Daily Bee*; December 28, 1895

579 *The Evening World Herald*, December 14, 1895

580 *The Omaha Daily Bee*; December 28, 1895

581 *The Omaha Daily Bee*; May 1, 1895

582 *The Evening World-Herald*, December 14, 1895 and *The Omaha Daily Bee*; December 14, 1895

583 *The Evening World-Herald*, December 16, 1895

584 *The Evening World-Herald*, December 16, 1895

585 *The Evening World-Herald*, December 18, 1895

586 Personal Knowledge of the writer

587 Hoover v. State; 48 Neb. 184, 66 N. W. 1117

588 *The Omaha Daily Bee*; December 27, 1895

589 *The Omaha Daily Bee*; December 28, 1895

590 *The Omaha Daily Bee*; December 28, 1895

591 *The Omaha Daily Bee*; December 30, 1895

592 *The Omaha Daily Bee*; December 30, 1895

593 *The Evening World-Herald*, February 12, 1896

594 *The Evening World-Herald*, February 19, 1896

595 Hoover v. State; 48 Neb. 184, 66 N. W. 1117

596 Hoover v. State; 48 Neb. 184, 66 N. W. 1117

597 Hoover v. State; 48 Neb. 184, 66 N. W. 1117

598 *The Evening World-Herald*, May 6, 1896

599 *The Evening World-Herald*, June 3, 1896

600 *The Evening World-Herald*, July 13, 1896

601 *The Omaha Daily Bee*; August 4, 1896

602 *The Evening World-Herald*, August 7, 1896

603 *The Omaha Daily Bee*; August 4, 1896

604 *The Omaha Daily Bee*; August 4, 1896

605 *The Evening World-Herald*, August 6, 1896

606 *The Evening World-Herald*, August 7, 1896

607 *The Omaha Daily Bee*; August 8, 1896

608 *The Omaha Daily Bee*; August 8, 1896

609 *The Evening World-Herald*, August 7, 1896

610 *The Omaha Daily Bee*; August 8, 1896

611 *The Omaha Daily Bee*; August 8, 1896

612 Records of Laurel Hill Cemetery; Omaha Public Library; Reference Section

613 *The Omaha Daily Bee*; August 12, 1896

614 *The Omaha Daily Bee*; March 16, 1901 & *The Custer County Republican*; June 17, 1909

615 *The Evening World-Herald*, November 4, 1895

616 *The Omaha Daily Bee*; November 4, 1895

617 *The Evening World-Herald*, November 4, 1895

618 *The Omaha Daily Bee*; November 4, 1895

619 *The Omaha Daily Bee*; November 4, 1895

620 *The Evening World-Herald*, November 4, 1895

621 Morgan v. State; 51 Neb. 672, 71 N.W. 788

622 *The Evening World-Herald*, November 4, 1895

623 *The Omaha Daily Bee*; November 4, 1895

624 *The Evening World-Herald*, November 4, 1895

625 *The Evening World-Herald*, November 4, 1895

626 *The Evening World-Herald*, November 4, 1895

627 *The Evening World-Herald*, November 4, 1895

628 Morgan v. State; 51 Neb. 672, 71 N.W. 788

629 *The Evening World-Herald*, November 4, 1895

630 *The Evening World-Herald*, November 4, 1895

631 *The Evening World-Herald*, November 7, 1895

632 *The Evening World -erald*, November 7, 1895

633 *The Omaha Daily Bee*; November 5, 1895

634 *The Omaha Daily Bee*; November 5, 1895

635 *The Omaha Daily Bee*; November 5, 1895

636 *The Omaha Daily Bee*; November 5, 1895

637 *The Omaha Daily Bee*; November 5, 1895

638 *The Evening World-Herald*, November 7, 1895 & *History at a Glance*; Douglas County Historical Society; Author Liz Rea, Director of Education; p. 40

639 *The Evening World-Herald*, November 7, 1895

640 *The Evening World-Herald*, November 7, 1895

641 *The Evening World-Herald*, November 11, 1895

642 *The Evening World-Herald*, November 18, 1895

643 *The Evening World-Herald*, November 23, 1895 & *The Omaha Daily Bee*; November 24, 1895

644 *The Evening World-Herald*, November 29 and 30, 1895

645 *The Evening World-Herald*, December 2, 1895

646 *The Evening World-Herald*, December 2, 1895 & *The Omaha Daily Bee*; December 3, 1895

647 *The Evening World-Herald*, December 3, 1895

648 *The Evening World-Herald*, December 4, 1895

649 *The Evening World-Herald*, November 29, 1895

650 *The Evening World-Herald*, December 5, 1895

651 *The Evening World-Herald*, December 5, 1895

652 *The Evening World-Herald*, December 5, 1895

653 *The Evening World-Herald*, December 6, 1895

654 *The Evening World-Herald*, December 7, 1895

655 *The Evening World-Herald*, December 9, 1895

656 *The Omaha Daily Bee*; December 9, 1895

657 *The Evening World-Herald*, December 9, 1895

658 *The Omaha Daily Bee*; December 22, 1895

659 *The Omaha Daily Bee*; December 22, 1895 & *The Evening World Herald*, December 21, 1895

660 *The Evening World-Herald*, December 28,1895

661 *The Evening World-Herald*, January 22, 1896

662 *The Evening World-Herald*, April 17, 1896

663 *The Evening World-Herald*, May 6, 1896

664 Morgan v. State; 51 Neb. 672, 71 N.W. 788; 1897

665 *The Evening World-Herald*, June 3 1897

666 *The Evening World-Herald*, September 28, 1897

667 *The Evening World-Herald*, September 28, 1897 & *The Evening World Herald*, October 1, 1897

668 *The Omaha Daily Bee*; October 7, 1897

669 *The Evening World-Herald*, October 6, 1897

670 *The Evening World-Herald*, October 7, 1897

671 *The Evening World-Herald*, October 8, 1897

672 *The Omaha Daily Bee*; October 9, 1897

673 *The Evening World-Herald*, October 8, 1897

674 *The Evening World-Herald*, October 8, 1897

675 *The Omaha Daily Bee*; October 9, 1897

676 *The Evening World-Herald*, October 8, 1897

677 *The Omaha Daily Bee*; October 9, 1897

678 *The Evening World-Herald*, October 8, 1897

679 *The Omaha Daily Bee*; October 9, 1897

680 *The Evening World-Herald*, October 8, 1897

681 *The Evening World-Herald*, October 9, 1897

682 *The Evening World-Herald*, October 12, 1897

683 *The Evening World-Herald*, October 8, 1897

684 *The Evening World-Herald*, October 8, 1897

685 *The Evening World Herald*, October 8, 1897

686 *The Omaha Daily Bee*; October 9, 1897

687   *The Evening World-Herald*, October 9, 1897 & *The Evening World Herald*, October 12, 1897

688 *The Evening World-Herald*, March 7 & 28, 1895

689 *The Norfolk News*, September 12, 1901 & *The Norfolk News*, September 12, 1901 & *Custer County Republican,* March 19, 1903

690 *The Evening World-Herald*, March 4, 1903

691 *The Evening World-Herald*, March 10, 1903

692 *The Evening World-Herald*, March 10, 1903

693 *The Evening World-Herald*, March 10, 1903

694 *The Evening World-Herald*, March 11, 1903

695 *Custer County Republican,* March 19, 1903

696 Records of the Nebraska Department of Corrections

697 Nebraska Revised Statutes, 1913, 9218 §643

INDEX